From Cover Girl to Cookie Queen

From Cover Girl to Cookie Queen

LIFE INGREDIENTS & RECIPES TO SATISFY
YOUR SWEET TOOTH & YOUR SOUL

LORI NADER GRAY

*Founder of Lori's Legendary Cookies
and Blue Chip Cookies*

HIGHERLIFE
DEVELOPMENT SERVICES, INC

Oviedo, Florida

From Cover Girl to Cookie Queen—Life Ingredients & Recipes To Satisfy Your Sweet Tooth & Your Soul
by Lori Nader Gray

Published by HigherLife Development Services, Inc.
400 Fontana Circle
Building 1—Suite 105
Oviedo, Florida 32765
(407) 563-4806
www.ahigherlife.com

ISBN 13: 978-1-935245-20-9
ISBN 10: 1-935245-20-9

Cover Design: Monster Design Company – Tom Beauchamp

First Edition
10 11 12 13 — 9 8 7 6 5 4 3 2 1
Printed in the United States of America

I dedicate this book to
my beautiful daughters,
Adele and Lindsay.

TABLE OF CONTENTS

INTRODUCTION

How does one go from Cover Girl makeup teen model to world famous store cookie magnate to abused wife to struggling single mom, and finally to learning what it takes to create a soul-satisfying, sweet life worth sharing?

You're about to find out.

From Cover Girl to Cookie Queen proves that anyone can rise again after being pushed down, flattened, and set aside. Just as baking soda and baking powder are added to cookie dough, leavening makes the difference between rising, falling, or flopping. And it's the temperature and quality of ingredients that determine the texture and taste to make baked goods soft and chewy—or doughy, flat, and tasteless.

Baking is about chemistry, and a cookie recipe must be formulated with precision and care. Sometimes it can take years of practice and many disappointments before we discover the perfect combination for a delicious recipe or a successful life, as in my case. Just when I'd think I had perfected my recipe, things beyond my control threw everything off kilter: ovens broke, eggs froze, butter and vanilla prices tripled, and hundreds of pounds of chocolate chips melted together into one giant chocolate drop!

Then after I fixed and remixed it all, a lawsuit, divorce, death, and job loss threatened to embitter me.

The leavening that lifted my soul and the antidote that saved my poisoned spirit was hope. But it took years of subtracting, re-measuring, re-sifting, and substituting key ingredients to create the recipes for the sweet life I enjoy today. These key ingredients have been folded into *From Cover Girl to Cookie Queen* with tasty, interesting true-life lessons packed into each chapter.

Like cookies, life comes in many flavors and varieties. And just as we require certain ingredients to create a stupendous cookie recipe, certain qualities must combine to create an outstanding life.

In this book you will enjoy a smorgasbord of these qualities from discipline and passion to gratitude and love. At the end of each chapter, you'll find a mouth-watering cookie recipe named for the chapter's life ingredient.

Should you decide to try each recipe and munch your way through the book, I hope the lessons learned will become baked into your soul, and every time you eat one of the cookies that lesson will come to mind. I believe in positive enforcement, and what better way to reinforce knowledge than through unimaginably delectable cookies?

With each chapter I have included morsels of truth—famous and not-so-famous inspirational quotes for you to digest. However, I do take full credit for: ***Red flags never change their color***; ***The longer you're single, the bigger your cojones***; and ***When life hands*** *you lemons, make lemon bars.* These are some of my personal favorites and have come to me from a half century of wisdom. You may quote me if you decide to write your own book one day.

Everything that you will read in the following pages exists to help you discover the necessary ingredients for your own personal recipe. The events and stories are not all chronological, but they really did happen. Some names and details have been changed to protect the innocent and not-so-innocent. It's not so much the events that are important, but the lessons learned from the events.

I really did party with the mayor of San Francisco, Tony Bennett, Joe Montana and Jay Leno. I did swim with the whales and win the Cover Girl model contest. I do live on Hope Lane, I am a certified scuba diver, and I did climb a twenty-foot tree in my late forties. I did marry twice before meeting my husband on Match.com (and those really are our profiles). I did found Blue Chip Cookies and create the very first White Chocolate Macadamia Nut cookie in1983, which changed cookie history. I was sued by a cookie giant, a massive cookie conglomerate to whom Blue Chip was a veritable speck on the radar in terms of cookie sales.

While I will not use their actual business name, it should be noted this cookie empire was always touting how their cookies made you "feel" and heretofore will be referred to as "Mrs. Feels." I do create my own fabulous cookie recipes and desserts from scratch, and I have the cellulite to prove it!

During my life of just over a half a century, I've discovered that life's lessons are constantly swirling invisibly around us, and often appear only when we are ready to recognize and embrace them.

From my experience, the lessons we need to learn most are usually the lessons we avoid, repeat, or run from. Take it from me, you will never outrun your lesson, so don't even bother trying!

It is my hope that by sharing my sweet and savory stories, you will pursue your passion, develop discipline, ground your faith, accept forgiveness, create courage, become balanced, live in gratitude, maintain your sense of humor no matter what, find love, and never, ever give up hope.

FROM LIFEGUARD
TO COVER GIRL

Discipline is the bridge between goals and accomplishment.

— Jim Rohn [1]

It's a Catch-22. You cannot learn discipline if you never challenge yourself. And you cannot take on new challenge if you do not become disciplined. "No pain, no gain" is part of living to our fullest potential. There is a long-term value that comes from discipline: confidence and a sense of control over your life—knowing you can take on a new job, start a new business, lose weight, or get to the finish line. It won't be easy. There will be struggles, setbacks, and unforeseen delays—but the payoff is worth every bit of blood, sweat, and tears you shed in getting there.

The telegram arrived on May 11, 1973. Cover Girl had selected me as the regional winner representing the West Coast and Canada. I couldn't believe I had been chosen as the new fresh face of one of the largest cosmetic companies in the world. My efforts had paid off, and I felt like the luckiest freshman girl in high school. No longer standing on the sidelines and daydreaming about a glamorous life in the fast lane, I was in the front seat, headed to the ball! Was it luck? My girl-next-door smile? The discipline I learned as a young girl? Most likely, it was all three.

My parents instilled in my older sister, younger brother, and me their strong work ethic from the time we were very young. I didn't grow up walking miles in the snow to school. I grew up appreciating the value of self-discipline. We all had responsibilities. My mom and dad worked full time, so weekly Saturday chores for us kids included cleaning the two-story house my dad built for us in Walnut Creek, California. We became the "Clean Team," vacuuming the carpet, mopping the hardwood and vinyl floors, cleaning the bathrooms, dusting all the furniture, and then cleaning our swimming pool. We didn't have a cleaning service or a pool sweep…we were it!

Many times I felt like Cinderella as I watched my friends, who didn't know the meaning of chores and who had weekly housekeepers or pool service, going off to the mall and having a ball without me.

During the summer, the "Clean Team" also had the privilege of pulling monstrous weeds that came back year after year on our half-acre, laboring in the hot sun if we slept too late. Helping can our fresh garden tomatoes and pick fruit from our apricot, peach, pear and apple trees were also part of our summer duties. We were not allowed any social time until we completed our chores and homework, so I learned to get up early and get going in the morning so I could meet my friends later at the mall. My parents were very fair and worked side by side with us, rewarding us with an allowance each week according to the chores we had accomplished. No work meant no pay and no play!

My mom and dad are opposites. While I was growing up, my mom, Shirley, worked as a secretary; my dad, Lyle, who was famous for his bow ties and crew cut, was known as "Mr. G" and taught chemistry at our local high school. Mom never brought her job home. An eternal optimist, she avoided confrontation and didn't stress about anything except a clean house and perfect entertaining. She always saw the possibilities in any situation. Her glass was three-quarters full. My dad, on the other hand, approached life pragmatically, and his scientific mind dictated that he live by facts, not feelings. He was from the old school of discipline, sacrifice, and "hard work never killed anyone." My dad was one of the most revered teachers at our high school—respected and feared by many of my friends, both male and female. Dad never lived outside his means and would only fulfill his dreams if they could be paid for with cash. If he couldn't see it, he couldn't dream it, and the extra jobs he held after school as the Drivers' Ed teacher and the wrestling, football, baseball, and basketball coach left little time for dreaming.

As the middle child, I became a blend of both Mom and Dad. Although practical like my dad, I had optimistic dreams and aspirations beyond my years of creating an extraordinary life looking at life through rose-colored glasses. I believed hard work, combined with dreams and optimism, would lead to a sweet life of "happily ever after."

The sweet life I sought would provide money for clothes that weren't on sale, a brand new car, vacations without sleeping bags, and a job I loved without working twenty-four-seven like my dad. "We can't afford it," "Money doesn't grow on trees," "Why do you think they call it work?," and "Shirley, what's for dessert?" These words my brother, sister, and I heard every day from my dad.

When I turned thirteen, I landed my first real job during the summer teaching swimming to young children making one dollar and thirty-five cents an hour, which seemed lucrative compared to pulling weeds for fifty cents an hour. The following year, I took lifeguard training and delighted in earning two dollars an hour more, all the while thinking, "This is great! I can work on my suntan and my lemon juice highlights and get paid at the same time!" After a long, hot, boring summer of screaming kids, far too many sunburns, and "Marco Polo" ringing in my ears, I decided to look for a more exciting vocation—one which did not require my nose to be covered in zinc oxide.

Lifeguard money in hand, I enrolled in an eight-week charm school program at our local shopping mall. My instructor was Ms. Hanes. She was older than my mother and dressed like a trendy teenager in miniskirts, platform shoes, and false eyelashes that never stayed on. Ms. Hanes taught me and five other starry-eyed, pubescent girls to stand up straight, apply makeup, style our hair, and walk the runway like a model. For the next eight weeks I became fascinated and absorbed by the mystique of modeling, and for two magical hours each week I was able to imagine myself as a successful runway model instead of the tall, gangly, insecure fourteen-year-old girl I was.

Because I took my upcoming graduation fashion show very seriously, I practiced my runway walk with hips out and model pout throughout our kitchen and family room between setting the table and doing the dishes. My brother just laughed at me while my mom, dad, and sister occasionally glanced my way between the evening news, cooking, and doing homework.

WITH SELF-DISCIPLINE MOST ANYTHING IS POSSIBLE.
—THEODORE ROOSEVELT[2]

I knew I was ready. This was going to be my ticket to my dreams. My graduation day finally arrived, bringing with it swarms of butterflies in my stomach and droves of shoppers on that Saturday afternoon. The runway was set up in the middle of the shopping mall for all to see. My family and friends filled the front row. A photographer from the mall was set up at the end of the runway to take pictures as we modeled the latest fall fashions. The music commenced, and the lights dimmed. The spotlight was on Ms. Hanes as she announced, "I'd like to welcome everyone to our sixth annual Fall Fashion show featuring the 1970 graduates from my highly successful charm and finishing school. Our first model is Lori, from Walnut Creek."

When I heard my name, I nervously walked out from behind the curtain and quickly breezed up and down the catwalk as fast as possible in my first ensemble: a long Renaissance-style dress, platform shoes, and a flower wreath in my hair. Just praying that I wouldn't catch the hem of dress with my heel, I did a quick turn and got off the runway—forgetting to pose for the photographer!

During my second appearance and with fewer butterflies, I strutted out in a gaucho skirt, peasant blouse, and low riding boots. This time I lingered longer on the runway, twirling my fringed skirt and my long sun-streaked hair. I also remembered to pose for the photographer before leaving the stage. By my final ensemble my butterflies were completely gone, and I was ready for my finale: suede hot pants, ruffled poet blouse, and lace-up boots. I was having fun. As I danced up and down the runway, I was strutting and turning with abandon. My modeling debut was a success, and Ms. Hanes told my parents I was a natural. She encouraged them to get me signed up with the Brebner Modeling Agency in San Francisco as soon as possible so I could be exposed to national print and commercial opportunities.

The following week, my mom drove me to San Francisco to be interviewed by Ann Brebner, who signed me up and scheduled a professional photographer to shoot my Zed card, a headshot to leave on interviews. On it were my statistics including my height, weight, measurements, and shoe size. As soon as the card was ready, Brebner agents began calling me for job interviews. So while my friends were enjoying going to pep rallies, football games, and munching on fast food after school, my mom was driving me to the city for interviews. Mom waited in the car, plugging the meter or circling the city blocks while I checked in with receptionists, coordinators, and stylists—quickly trying on clothes and leaving my Zed card for their files.

I landed my first print modeling job with Levi Strauss at the age of fifteen. I was making fifty dollars an hour and I felt like I was rolling in money. I decided that depriving myself of food was worth every cent I earned. It had not been easy when my friends were chomping Big Macs and fries after school while I nibbled on twig-sized celery and carrot sticks. But the hardest part was being around my family, who believed that dessert was a food group and was necessary for each meal to be complete. I would not savor my homemade chocolate chip cookies for quite a while.

During my modeling high school years, I was naturally driven to excel and so I did everything I could to stand out in the crowd. I enjoyed experimenting behind the sewing machine in my home economics class, creating unique clothes and accessories I could wear for school or modeling interviews. Some of my creations included empire-line dresses with angel sleeves and high-waisted bell bottoms I had copied from the fashion magazines. I made macramé belts and velour hats covered in everything from fruit to feathers.

I decided to enter the "Make it With Wool" contest sponsored by Pendleton. I chose a complicated *Vogue* pattern that would challenge the likes of Martha Stewart. It included a fabulous cape-style, fully lined wool plaid jacket with fabric self-covered buttons, coordinating caramel cuffed trousers, and matching Bogart-style hat. I finished it, but by the time I had I was so sick of bound button holes, invisible zippers, and matching plaid cut on the bias, I never wanted to see a cape again! Modeling my lovely wool ensemble for the contest during one of the hottest days in the summer after being overbaked from too much sunbathing was the last thing I wanted to do! Strutting down the cat walk with hips forward and head back, I felt as stiff as the Tin Man, wincing with each stride and turn as I swirled my scratchy wool cape jacket to impress the judges—but I was smiling all the while through my pain. I won second place and ended my sewing career, happily retiring my sewing machine and eschewing anything made of wool for a very long time.

Still ready for another challenge, while I was perusing a fashion magazine I saw another contest. The Cover Girl cosmetic company was searching for its next High School Cover Girl model. All I had to do was send in one full-length and one close-up photo-graph of myself and describe in seventy-five words or less my daily grooming routine, including the beauty aids I considered most important. No sewing required! I decided a poem would be a unique way to stand out, and since the contest was sponsored by Noxzema, I highlighted that product. I guess I had a sense of marketing even at sixteen!

Here's what I wrote:

> *My daily routine of personal care*
> *Begins with a shower and ends with my hair.*

Lip gloss, mascara, blusher to face,
Soon I'll be ready to vie in the race.
For modeling requires special attention,
Like Cover Girl makeup, just thought I would mention.
Yes, these and exercise make for good looks,
So biking and swimming and hitting the books.
Then bedtime calls for full facial clearance,
Noxzema's a must for full bloom appearance!

After I received the winning telegram, I became an overnight star in my small suburban home town. Photographers from the local newspapers came to my house, and radio and TV stations broadcasted my story. My discipline was paying off, and I was about to realize my dream of the good life. The Noxzema company flew me to New York City for the final competition. When I arrived, a team of photographers snapped my picture, and a limousine with a chauffeur named William awaited me.

As William opened my limo door, I felt like a true celebrity. I couldn't wait to tell my friends and family back home! From the first class flight to the accommodations at the Waldorf Astoria—a hotel I had only heard about in the movies—all of it was better than any sugar rush I had ever experienced. My red carpet treatment included five-star restaurants and Broadway shows, such as *Pippin* and *Irene*, which included a backstage meeting with Debbie Reynolds, a famous singer, dancer, and movie star.

At night I danced at the hippest discos in New York. During the day I toured the Museum of Modern Art and the United Nations building. From wardrobe fittings to hair styling, I was booked every hour of every day for six days. I became utterly intoxicated with this sweet life. In my heart I knew it wasn't the modeling that I loved, it was the recognition and how special it made me feel. The potential to make the kind of money successful models made was as enticing and as addicting as sugar to me.

With my new Cover Girl makeover and shorter hair, dressed up in my paisley minidress and knee-high boots, I was ready for the cocktail party Noxzema hosted at the Waldorf to introduce the five regional winners to the press and talent scouts from top modeling agencies in New York. Throughout the evening, I schmoozed and made small talk about being a California girl, all the while thinking about home sweet home and the chocolate chip cookies I was planning to make and devour when I got home.

Early the following morning, my hotel phone rang incessantly until I finally picked it up and sleepily said, "Hello." It was someone I had met at the party from Wilhelmina Models, one of the top modeling firms in the world. He was calling on behalf of Wilhelmina, who wanted an interview with me that day. Feeling nervous and excited, I accepted the appointment and scrambled to get ready.

It was my last day in New York, so instead of enjoying the shopping spree I had planned at Bloomingdale's with the other contestants and the humongous corned beef sandwich and famous New York cheesecake from The Carnegie Deli, I caught the bus to Park Avenue.

When the elevator reached my stop at the top floor, I was overwhelmed when I entered the expansive reception area, which looked more like a posh hotel lobby. Dramatic oversized flower-arrangements were strategically placed on exquisite tables. Bronze sculptures and antique chairs were sitting on Persian rugs. Beautiful, famous faces I recognized from fashion magazines smiled at me from the frames that covered the walls. As I waited, I watched models come and go, feeling somewhat awed by how skinny and even more gorgeous they were in person. What was I doing there? Then, just like Dorothy from *The Wizard of Oz*, I told myself that I was not in Kansas (Walnut Creek) anymore.

Just then a statuesque, bone-thin older woman came out and introduced herself asWilhelmina. She walked me into her office overlooking Manhattan, and after I had gasped at the splendor of the urban landscape below, my eyes became fixed on the magazine covers that covered her wall—all with her photo on the front. Hers had once been one of the most famous faces in the world.

After chatting a while with me about my experience in New York to put me at ease, Wilhelmina asked me whether I would consider coming back in July to model for her agency for the summer. Without even thinking I replied "Yes, if my parents agree."

She immediately picked up her gold designer phone with her long, perfectly manicured nails. "Let's call them, and I'll explain all the details."

Wilhelmina told my parents she would arrange everything, from my locating an apartment to finding suitable roommates for me. She assured my parents that she would personally watch out for me, and she went on to explain to them how this rare opportunity could launch my career in modeling. After much discussion and still no definite decision, Wilhelmina hung up the phone. Then, piercing me with her steel blue eyes, she told me she needed me to do one thing if I returned.

"Anything," I said, and I meant it. Who wouldn't do anything to be represented by one of the world's top agencies? They've represented some of the most beautiful models and actresses alive.

"You need to lose eight pounds. I want you under a hundred and twenty pounds before I send you out on interviews."

Piece of cake. I was already considered thin, but if Wilhelmina wanted me skeletal, I could definitely lose eight pounds over the next six weeks.

During my first-class flight home, I ate everything offered to me, starting with the cheese plate and finishing with the chocolate mousse—resolving to start my weight loss regime the next morning. That was when I would have to face the even bigger challenge of convincing my mom and especially my dad that New York was my opportunity of a lifetime and my chance to go the ball and try on the glass slipper!

Once I was back home, my parents thought I would forget about New York. But getting back there was all I thought about and talked about. Even as responsible as I was, my parents were not comfortable with me living in New York on my own. The answer was still NO.

I began my strict dieting regime anyway, hoping they would eventually change their minds. My parents knew how determined I could be when I wanted something, and they watched as I endured the grapefruit diet, fish diet, pineapple diet and protein diet. I ate canned tuna and tomato juice for breakfast while they gobbled strawberry waffles and chocolate chip pancakes smothered in maple syrup, and for dinner as they indulged in meatloaf, mashed potatoes and gravy topped off with homemade apple pie a la mode. Meanwhile, I was eating skinless broiled chicken and salad sprinkled with lemon juice, then splurging with sugar-free Jell-O for dessert and feeling very virtuous...and determined to go back to NYC.

THE ABILITY TO DISCIPLINE YOURSELF TO DELAY GRATIFICATION IN THE SHORT TERM IN ORDER TO ENJOY GREATER REWARDS IN THE LONG TERM, IS THE INDISPENSABLE PREREQUISITE FOR SUCCESS.

—BRIAN TRACY[3]

Weekends were especially hard, with the aroma of juicy grilled cheeseburgers, gooey potato salad and corn on the cob slathered in butter as I ate a plain hamburger with lettuce sans the bun and cheese. And our Sunday barbecues were not complete without Mom's homemade fudge sauce poured over ice cream covered with marshmallows and toasted almonds, which everyone else devoured...as I ate more sugar free Jell-O.

Calculating the calorie count of everything before I put it into my mouth, I swam laps in our pool to burn off any excess calories, sometimes swimming twice a day. I was determined to reach my goal and to go back to New York with my hip bones sticking out.

About a month of being home and losing six pounds, I received a call from Wilhelmina to check in with me and my parents. With my parents on their phone in the bedroom and me on the kitchen extension, Wilhelmina explained to us that she needed to start making living arrangements for me if I planned to return to New York for the summer. My parents began asking her more questions about my safety and supervision, and Wilhelmina constantly reassured them that she would watch over me. She told them I would be rooming with two mature models in their twenties who had been living in New York for the past year. She emphasized to my parents how marketable my fresh California look was and how the money I could make as a model would help with any college plans as well as open many doors for me in the future. I heard my mom agreeing and then I heard my dad agreeing with her reluctantly. "I guess she can go." I screamed with glee from the kitchen, and to celebrate I baked my favorite chocolate chip cookies and ate enough cookies and dough to gain back almost two pounds!

Back to my dieting regime I went. Six weeks later I was on my way back to New York, only this time seated in the coach section.

When I arrived at the airport, there were no limousines or photographers waiting for me. Instead I was met by someone from the agency, and we took a wild taxi ride to a noisy, old hotel on the West Side of Manhattan. The only comforting part was knowing the doorman Alfred was out front guarding our building. I had been so excited to be back in New York after accomplishing my painstaking goal. But inside I felt let down by the less-than-welcoming accommodations.

Not only was this a huge contrast from my previous visit, it was not nearly what I had expected. I never let on to my parents that I was not completely happy when I called them each day. For the next two and a half months, this noisy two-bedroom apartment with worn green carpeting, faded drapes, and dim lighting was to become my home.

I hoped I would become friends with my new roommates. Nikki was from the Midwest and immediately made me feel welcome. We shared the larger room and also a love for family, our dogs, and going to the movies. Beverly Hills-bred Joan barely spoke to me and treated me like the little sister and a third wheel. She was aloof and did not have any desire to connect with me. Nikki became like a big sister, introducing me to vintage clothes, amazing fashion outlets in Brooklyn, and cheese blintzes.

Modeling in New York brought unimaginable culture shock. Getting lost on buses and subways and walking down dark hallways leading to freight elevators which would take me up to photographers' studios was very scary. My map became so well used, it was unreadable at the folds—not unlike the folds of my feet which became blistered from wearing the latest platform shoes for modeling jobs.

To get my career up and running and to introduce me as the hot new model in town, my agency booked eight to ten appointments each day. I rode buses and subways from one end of town to another. I had never worked so hard at becoming known in all my life, and I couldn't even reward myself with a sweet treat at the end of a hard day! Even Nikki's friendship and the occasional plate of cheese blintzes we shared couldn't come close to satisfying my chocolate chip cravings or my homesickness.

I finally got a lucky break when a famous photographer whose work had been featured in *Vogue* and *Bazaar* magazines requested a photo shoot with me. My booking agent was thrilled and emphasized what a great opportunity it was for me.

Arriving at the photographer's studio, my tote bag full of tricks in hand, I expected a makeup artist or stylist there to help me. There was no one in the studio but an older, overweight photographer with shoulder-length greasy hair and a scraggly goatee. I got to work getting ready for the shoot. The vast studio of "Mr. Grease" was impressive, and his makeup room was well organized, filled with thousands of dollars worth of makeup and accessories. The clothes I was wearing for the shoot hung neatly on rolling racks, waiting for me to don.

Led Zepplin was playing loudly. The photographer asked me if I would like anything to drink or smoke as he took a drag of his marijuana cigarette. I started feeling more and more uncomfortable. I requested water. Looking around, I realized that his bedroom and kitchen were adjacent to the area where we were going to shoot, which did little to allay my discomfort. But I knew that I had to go on as if nothing was at all unusual about the situation.

As I came out in my first outfit, a long halter dress, the photographer (who was high) told me I looked "hot" as he dimmed the lights. When he showed me the Polaroid of me he had taken of me to check the lighting, I couldn't believe how beautiful I looked. I told myself to relax and enjoy the shoot. When I put on the next outfit, a creamy blouse with exotic sleeves and matching bell-bottom pants pulled together with a giant gold belt and earrings, I felt like a *Vogue* magazine model.

Mr. Grease asked if I would lose my bra, using the excuse that it showed through the blouse. Nervous as I was, I took it off, and he began shooting full-length pictures in the studio. He then explained to me how he needed to capture a different look and feel, telling me that the lighting in his bedroom would be perfect. I was really feeling uncomfortable. As I sat on the bed, this guy began shooting what seemed like hundreds of pictures, all the while telling me over and over how beautiful I looked and that he couldn't believe I was only sixteen. He asked if I had a boyfriend. I immediately answered, "Yes, we've been together since sixth grade, he calls me every day and we'll probably get married." I was trying to sound mature, and I was also hoping my white lie would dissuade him from making any advances toward me. He then requested I unbutton one more button on my blouse, lean back, and act sexy and imagine that he was my boyfriend. (I have always had a great imagination, but that visual was impossible!) The most uncomfortable I had ever felt up till then was when I had gotten stuck on the freight elevator making my modeling rounds. This was too much. I wanted this photo shoot over that minute! I didn't care how great a photographer he was. He kept getting closer and closer to me as he kept shooting pictures, murmuring that he was getting really turned on. The next thing I knew, this greaseball was groping me and trying to kiss me—telling me I mustn't tease him!

I sprung up from his bed and ran to the dressing room and quickly changed. I was out of there without saying goodbye. I couldn't believe what had just happened. I had heard about such seduction attempts, but thought it only happened in the movies. No one had warned me how to cope with such a situation. Feeling embarrassed, I never told my agency about it.

When my photos arrived from the shoot, they were amazing. I looked like the models in the magazines—worldly, beautiful and sophisticated. The agency was so impressed, they continued booking me as their new "best-kept secret" from California. Little did they know.

After getting to know other models late that summer, I realized I was not the only one who had had such an experience. Just like in Hollywood, where actresses are expected to sink into the producers' couches, New York has many ensnaring photographers' studios for models.

For the rest of the summer, I worked with several more great photographers, and thankfully they were respectful and never came on to me. Even so, I feared and dreaded that other Mr. Greases were lying in wait with every shoot. I yearned to go home.

Only one time did Wilhelmina call me into her office to check how I was faring in New York. She invited me for a sushi dinner with four top models I recognized from the agency. It was my first raw fish experience, and I don't know if it was the intimidation I felt from being around those famous faces or the raw fish that caused me to lose my appetite. That was the extent of Wilhelmina's supervision during my stay in New York.

This had turned out to be one very long, hot, muggy, and bitter-sweet summer, and I couldn't wait for it to end. High school, homework, and weekly chores had never sounded so good. And I really missed my family. I was proud of myself for accomplishing my goal and surviving New York at sixteen, but my dreams were now of California and my chocolate chip cookies.

Once home with the New York experience and portfolio in hand, my modeling career really took off, and I began making lots of dough—even some of my favorite kind. Now and then after a modeling job, I rewarded myself by making my favorite chocolate chip cookies, often eating half the dough and diving into our pool to swim off what calories I could.

But the water in our swimming pool couldn't wash away the dirt my foray into New York modeling had imprinted on my psyche. Never feeling thin enough and being judged by the shape of my legs, the size of my teeth, and the color of my hair had taken a toll on my self-image and my sense of worth. I remembered the cattle calls, all of us gorgeous girls competing for the same TV commercial or print job, always hoping we'd be the chosen one. Fear of failure followed me like a ghost. I disciplined myself and tried not to look over my shoulder.

I continued going on interviews in San Francisco after school, but now I could drive myself into the city. Sometimes getting to the interview became the most challenging part, with driving up and down the hills of San Francisco in my old Volvo stick shift and teetering at the top of Nob Hill while waiting for cable cars to unload, all the while reading my folded city map. I headed up and down one-way streets, double parking in alleys, getting ticketed and sometimes towed.

I was seventeen when I landed my first of many television commercials, a high-paying national gig for swimsuits. I was excited not only by the attention but also because I needed every penny to put towards my college tuition. At the interview, The New York producer asked me how comfortable I was in large bodies of water. "And do you like to swim?"

I confidently answered, "I love to swim! I practically lived in our family pool and on the beach growing up. Besides, I'm a California girl and a certified lifeguard!"

Well, when the commercial coordinator told me to meet him at Marine World, I should have had a clue that this was not going to be an ordinary swimsuit commercial .

He told me not to worry—the photographer was going to shoot the commercial through the thick glass of the aquarium and the trainer would stand nearby. Meanwhile, I would be swimming underwater, smiling and posing like a mermaid to show off the coral-colored two-piece bathing suit covered with shimmering sea shells. There was just one small catch: I would have to swim in the large killer whale tank with the two killer whales in holding tanks on either side!

I was terrified. But it was too late to back out, and besides, I needed the money. I could hear the whales making loud noises and spouting off, which I interpreted as meaning that they weren't too happy about this foreign fish in their tank. I wasn't exactly thrilled with my work conditions—terror, whale poop, and freezing sea salt water. But the show had to go on, and so I smiled and swam and got out of there as fast as I could!

I survived the killer whales and laughed all the way home, and ever since. This made swimming with the dolphins look like a cake walk!

My first commercial opened doors to many others from Honda to Coca Cola, and to acting as an extra in a couple of movies, like *Snoopy Come Home,* where I worked with Charles Schultz, and *The Towering Inferno.* (I fell in love with Steve McQueen, though I never met him.)

I was introduced to discipline at an early age, but was introduced to a life of glamour and the sweet spoils of success while I was in high school. With the discipline and hard-work ethic I learned as a child, I never feared new challenges, and I always set ambitious goals. Meeting each challenge helped me develop more discipline, self-confidence, and organizational skills.

I am still learning the discipline of discipline. The more I practice, the easier it gets!

LORI GEERTSON

Cover Girl finalist

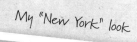

My "New York" look

A glamour shot

LIFE INGREDIENT: DISCIPLINE
MACADAMIA SURPRISE DE LITES*

⅔ cup macadamia nuts
½ cup granulated sugar
½ cup light brown sugar
1 teaspoon vanilla extract
1 large egg
1 ¼ cups all-purpose flour
½ teaspoon baking soda

¼ teaspoon salt
½ cup dried cranberries
½ cup white chocolate chips (optional)
⅛ cup finely chopped coconut (optional)

➤ Preheat oven to 350 degrees.
➤ Place nuts in a food processor and process until it becomes like butter and smooth (about 2 minutes).
➤ Combine macadamia butter and sugars in mixing bowl; beat with a mixer at medium speed.
➤ Add vanilla and egg. Beat well.
➤ Measure out flour and level with knife. Combine flour, baking soda, and salt; stir with a whisk.
➤ Gradually add flour mixture to macadamia butter mixture. Stir to combine.
➤ Add coconut, cranberries, and white chocolate chips.
➤ Chill dough for 10 minutes.
➤ Roll into 1" dough balls, place onto parchment-lined baking sheet, and slightly flatten each ball with the palm of your hand.
➤ Bake for 12-14 minutes or until lightly golden.
➤ Remove from cookie sheet and cool on wire rack.

*There is no butter in this cookie!

Makes approximately 30 cookies.

THE SUGAR RUSH THAT LED TO THE SWEET LIFE!

Passion requires focused direction, and that direction must come from three other areas: your purpose, your talents, and your needs.

—Steve Pavlina[4]

Nothing beats the feeling of doing what you love. Find out what you love and explore every opportunity to express it. It doesn't mean you have to start your own business, but the more closely your life's activities parallel what you truly enjoy doing, the more contented you'll feel inside. We all have passions within us, and the key is to identify yours and then spend as much time as possible living well and expressing it!

My passion for cookies started in our kitchen at home, where my family's love of dessert was indulged every night. My mom always created something delicious every day, but she was best known for her homemade pies and cakes, especially her carrot cake and her lemon meringue and coconut cream pies. The rest of the family joined in the sugar parade as well. My sister made fantastic cinnamon rolls and brownies with gooey frosting, my dad's specialty was his two-flavor fudge, and my brother was the muffin maker (but he was mainly our sample taster). Because cookies were so quick and easy to make, they became my specialty.

I was best known for my mouthwatering gourmet chocolate chip, oatmeal, and sugar cookies, all made with my secret ingredient, which made them soft and chewy in the center with light, crusty edges.

Everything was always made from scratch, with lots of butter, sugar, and love. Our family desserts seemed to have the power to make my sister, brother, and me feel happy, content and connected, especially to Mom and Dad as we sat around the kitchen table together, laughing and talking with mouthfuls of delectable delights. Just knowing there was something sweet for dessert always put a smile on my dad's sometimes sour face and made him act like a kid in a candy store. And if Dad was happy, we all were happy! Desserts were our sweet refuge after a hard day at work or school.

After happily retiring my sewing machine, I began manning the mixing bowl in my home economics class. I created scrumptious treats to share with my family and friends. Advanced Home Ec took me to the next level and was not only my favorite class, it was the only one in which I earned consistent A's.

Because of the Cover Girl contest win, my modeling and commercial work during high school provided me the means to attend the University of California in Los Angeles (UCLA), where I continued to model. This was during the 1970s, and while my college friends were waiting tables at minimum wage, I was making between seventy-five and one hundred fifty dollars an hour, which allowed me to pay for college with just enough left over to whet my appetite by enabling me to drive a BMW, wear designer clothes, and buy expensive gifts for my family and friends. For Mother's Day, I flew my mom down to LA and treated her to a makeover at Jon Peters Salon. Three swishy stylists washed, cut, and transformed her hair and makeup. I was bound and determined she throw away her bedtime curlers. Looking fabulous and feeling exhilarated, we shopped on Rodeo Drive and then dined at The Palm restaurant, where we topped off dinner with mouthwatering cheesecake. Charlton Heston dined at the table next to us, which thrilled my mom since he was one of her favorite actors. It was a perfectly sweet day for both of us, and one I will always cherish.

I continued modeling through college. Between my work and my studies, there wasn't much time to make cookies; plus, cookies and modeling were not compatible in my world. I was not naturally skinny, and since I loved food and had an insatiable sweet tooth, I was always dieting. Now and then, if I was feeling thin enough and didn't have any swimsuit jobs coming up, I would justify buying cookies from the Famous Amos cookie store on

Sunset Boulevard. I knew if I mixed cookie dough from scratch I would eat most of the dough plus too many cookies and then end up feeling sick, guilty, and fat.

At Famous Amos, Wally Amos himself waited on me many times. He was always laughing and smiling, and everyone who bought cookies at his store seemed happy as well. It reminded me how I felt at home when my family and I were eating desserts together. I was amazed to see how many people had a sweet tooth like mine, and even more surprised to see how many people wanted to buy bags of freshly baked cookies from a cookie store at three times the price of a package of Chips Ahoy. I couldn't imagine why. Didn't people know how to bake?

I knew in my heart that modeling would not be my life's work, because it involved riding too many emotional waves, like a sugar high followed by a sugar crash. Driving hours through Los Angeles traffic and then waiting up to an hour with fifty other gorgeous girls for a five-minute interview was exhausting. Watching a photographer or art director flip through the pages of my port-folio as if speed reading and then hearing, "We'll call you. Next!" was humiliating. Being judged solely on my looks and treated like a commodity was not great for my self esteem, my heart, or my soul. But rejection was part of the business, and I had to develop a thick crust on the outside to hide the fact that I was many times crumbling like buttery shortbread on the inside.

There were some great highs, like the trips to Acapulco and Puerta Vallarta for swimsuit catalogs and to Sun Valley, Idaho, for ski wear, where I met the Winston cigarette man, whom I recognized from seeing his face plastered on billboards all over L.A. He was European, fluent in many languages, and had an English accent—tall and tan with a chiseled face, a gorgeous athletic body, and thick brown hair. His accent excited me, and his sophistication intoxicated me. The only negative I could see was his habit of smoking, which I quickly overlooked, so I began dating him. He was here from Britain and was determined, like every other model, to become a famous actor. Listening to the waves at his Malibu Beach bungalow and his sexy accent was all it took for me to fall head over heels in love for the first time. I was twenty years old.

One morning we were getting ready to meet a few of his actor friends for brunch when a call came in. He picked up the phone and started speaking German to someone I could tell he knew very intimately. When he got off the phone I asked him, "Who was that?"

"That was my wife and little boy and girl calling from Germany." He was so casual in his response. "Are you ready to go?"

My mouth dropped. "Are you saying you're married, and you have children? Why in the world are you dating me, and why didn't you tell me you were married?"

He proceeded to tell me that he and his wife had an open arrangement for years, and that it was no big deal for them to date or sleep with other people.

So much for the delicious brunch I was about to enjoy at the Beverly Hills Hotel...and their Eggs Benedict and mimosas had been calling my name! I left that morning, feeling totally disillusioned about love. I never saw him again, except plastered all over Los Angeles billboards while I would be driving down Sunset Boulevard on the way to Famous Amos for my cookie fix. That Englishman was not the "happily ever after" I was looking for, but he was the first and last model I ever dated. He was not the last Englishman in my life, however.

After graduating from UCLA, I moved to San Francisco with my best friend and college roommate, Carmel. We lived in an art deco apartment on the edge of Pacific Heights where we had not only had a killer vista view of the Bay, but also we felt on top of the world. *Now what?* I had never really thought about a career, and although I had a BA degree in sociology, I had no idea what to do with it.

THE GREATER DANGER FOR MOST OF US LIES NOT IN SETTING OUR AIM TOO HIGH AND FALLING SHORT; BUT IN SETTING OUR AIM TOO LOW AND ACHIEVING OUR MARK.
—MICHELANGELO[5]

I continued modeling, and when I started being cast as a mom or bride in many of the print ads, and finally a pregnant wife wearing a fake baby bulge, I knew I was getting too old for the business. My modeling career was rapidly losing its appeal.

I thought that I could always become a teacher like my dad, and teaching would fit in nicely with my dream of having a family. But I realized the salary would never afford me the rich lifestyle I had developed a taste for.

Because my modeling jobs became fewer and farther apart, I decided to get a job working nine to five at the largest modeling school in San Francisco. I landed a position as an instructor, teaching young girls about the glamorous world of modeling. The pay was steady, and they allowed me time off to work in the modeling jobs I got called for now and then.

As I watched the slimy salespeople enroll hundreds of starry-eyed young girls in their school, promising these innocents they could be the next top model or actress as their parents signed contracts for thousands of dollars, it broke my heart. Many of these young girls were extremely overweight, some riddled with acne and some just over five feet tall. While I was instructing, I played down the modeling and worked on building their confidence and self-esteem, telling them about exciting behind-the-scene job opportunities in the acting industry. Trying not to give them false hope, I still came home at the end of each day with a bad taste in my mouth, somewhat like biting into a cheap cookie made with rancid shortening. I hated the job, but I needed to make a steady living. San Francisco and the sweet life I aspired to came at a high price.

Deep inside what I really wanted was to get married and start a family. I was now twenty-two years old, and many of my high school friends were already married. I started looking for my Prince Charming at the city's hottest bars and disco clubs. Thursday evenings after work, Carmel and I hung out at Perry's on Union Street, the sports bar for the hip after work crowd who drank wine and nibbled on the signature breadsticks, and then danced the night away at the private discotheque Mumm's, with its floor-to-ceiling mirrors. The champagne and cocaine flowed freely, and it was fun and exciting for a while. With our L.A. style of dress and youthful beauty, we turned heads wherever we went. Expensive silks, hot designer stilettos, and the tightest jeans we could fit into made us irresistible. We also exuded an air of confidence and were often the youngest girls in the room. Wherever we went, we stood out in the crowd, and we loved it. I was the sexy blond bombshell, and Carmel was the cute brunette beauty. We looked like player types, but inside we were both conservative country girls looking for "happily ever after." Hanging around the older crowd made me feel mature and grown up. I was searching for someone successful, established, and in control. But I would soon understand all too well the adage, "Be careful what you wish for!"

One evening Carmel and I decided to splurge on dinner at Perry's Restaurant. We were both very frugal when it came to dining out, and we were always on a diet. Saving for our designer clothes seemed far more important and offered a much better return than fine dining.

We had just sat down when a suave, charming, and much older man walked up to our table and introduced himself in a sexy accent as, "Marceem, but everyone calls me Marc." He was dressed to the nines in an Italian suit, open silk shirt, and crocodile tasseled shoes. He asked if he could join us for a drink but said he could not stay as he had another commitment. He added that he would be at Mumm's later on.

When the bill came, the waiter told us that it had been paid by one of his best customers. Carmel and I headed straight to Mumm's to see Marc. He was there, and flashed a smile when he saw us and signaled for us to join him at his table. As he made sure our glasses were overflowing with champagne, Marc danced with both of us all night, although I could tell he had eyes for me. I was very impressed. (This was so much better than the beer keg and chip-and-dip parties the frat boys hosted.)

Marc looked Middle Eastern and appeared too old for me, but there was something about him I was attracted to. His confidence and worldly manner intrigued me so much that I overlooked the chain smoking and all the scotch he consumed. He proudly told us he had lived in San Francisco since he was eighteen, when his parents sent him from Lebanon to attend San Francisco University. He currently was a manufacturer's representative traveling the world, though most of his business took place in the Middle East. By the way he dressed and the way he spent money on drinks for friends at the bar, Marc had the appearance of a successful man. But I could not help but notice how intimidating he became to the waiter if his drink took too long to arrive or his ashtray were not emptied in a timely manner. As we sat together, he joked with us in his thick accent, saying, "I've always said, you can't afford to drink if you have to count the glasses!" (At that time, I never realized how significant counting the glasses would become.) Once again Marc treated us to everything, including our valet parking. Before Carmel and I left Mumm's, Marc told me he would like to take me to dinner at his favorite Nob Hill restaurant and asked if I would go out with him the next Saturday night. Feeling flattered, I ignored the uneasiness I had about our differences, and I answered yes.

I was nervous as I got ready for my first date with Marc. There was mystique and intrigue about him, as well as something a bit daunting. He picked me up in his new black Jaguar, and we drove to the Top of The Mark. He tossed his keys to the valet as he grabbed my hand and escorted me to the best table in the house, with three-hundred-sixty-degree views of twinkling lights overlooking the city. Marc ordered for both of us. We started with a bottle of Cristal champagne and with it, my first taste of escargot.

Next was spinach bisque, followed by endive and watercress salad and then Beef Bourgogne with a bottle of Chateauneuf du Pape. After dinner, Marc lit a cigarette and ordered a snifter of aged cognac as I devoured the Grand Marnier Soufflé. It felt so exciting to be out with such a worldly and sophisticated man. And after our three-hour feast, I was feeling intoxicated not only by the first-class attention, but also the alcohol. All of a sudden our

CHOOSE A JOB YOU LOVE, AND YOU WILL NEVER HAVE TO WORK A DAY IN YOUR LIFE.

—CONFUCIUS[7]

sixteen-year age difference didn't seem like a problem. I agreed to another date. Over the next six months, Marc continued to wine and dine me and to seduce me with Cartier jewelry, French perfume, and cashmere for Christmas. I discovered he was an excellent cook when he introduced me to his favorite Middle

Eastern foods, which he delighted in sharing with my family (who weren't quite sure about our relationship).

I loved all the attention we attracted when we were together. Marc commanded respect mixed with fear wherever he went, and all the upper crust of San Francisco seemed to know him.

So when he asked me to move in with him, quit the job I hated, and let him take care of me, I exclaimed, "Yes!" I moved into his Pacific Heights high-rise, with its dramatic and enchanting views of the Golden Gate Bridge and Palace of Fine Arts, thrilled to be living the good life I had always aspired to.

My parents, however, were not as thrilled. They did not believe in living together and thought I was making a big mistake. "A man will never buy the cow when the milk is free," my dad pronounced.

Even though Marc had been generous and kind to me and my family, it did not stop the waving red flags: his age, his drinking and smoking, plus our cultural differences. But I was convinced those red flags could change colors. After all, doesn't love conquer all?

For the next year while we were living together, I witnessed and lived through Marc's drinking binges, angry explosions towards friends, foes, waiters, and even me if I questioned him. After investing a year with Marc, I still wasn't willing to face the failure I would feel if I were to leave the relationship and admit defeat. Plus, I had quit my job and lost my lease on the flat I had with Carmel. I had few options. I couldn't face the idea of moving back home, and I had no idea of what I would do or where I would live if I left Marc. At twenty-three years old, I made the brilliant decision to accept his marriage proposal. I didn't understand alcohol addiction and thought moving out of the city away from the night life and starting a family would solve our problems and mellow this hot-tempered Middle Eastern man. So I thought.

Planning our wedding and blending our beliefs and cultures was like trying to mix oil and water: if you shake it up hard enough, it will stay mixed for a while, but it soon separates. Marc's idea of a wedding was a big party with an abundance of the finest foods and libations. Mine was an intimate, spiritual time of connection and commitment with close family and friends. He was anti-religion and believed it caused the pain and suffering in most of the world—just look at his Lebanon. So completely compromising my faith and values, we were married by a justice of the peace at the very top of the St. Francis Hotel overlooking the city, at our favorite discothèque, Oz. It was Valentine's Day, 1981.

But it was anything but romantic. Marc arrived almost an hour late, extremely hung over from enjoying his wild bachelor party the night before. Angry and hurt while waiting for him to show up, I seriously thought about canceling our wedding. But insecurities and image controlled me, and after all, what would our guests think? So the show went on. And quite a show it was, with twinkling white lights, red and white long-stemmed roses, panoramic views of the city, and an abundance of the finest food and champagne! It was a beautiful party for my family and our friends, although I don't think Marc remembered much of it. He wore large, dark glasses, covering half his face in many of our wedding pictures. Marc's family was not in attendance. Because they all lived in Lebanon, they wished us congratulations by phone in Arabic. (Although I never knew if they were wishing me well or cursing me out.)

Being married didn't change anything, except my name. And getting married on the most romantic Hallmark holiday did nothing to stop the waving red flags, which were still red as a setting sun in smog. The five-star dining, the recreational drugs, and the emptiness of shopping began losing their flavor. Being taken care of felt more like being controlled, and I quickly began to feel more like a prisoner in a castle with walls than a new happily married bride.

Adjusting to life with a man who was deathly allergic to eggs and who loved cooked fava beans and pita bread for breakfast was challenging. No scrambled eggs, waffles and chocolate chip pancakes, and certainly no homemade cookies for him! His Middle Eastern diet was great now and then, but I just couldn't stomach eating it daily, let alone three times a day! As a California girl, I loved American, Mexican, Chinese, and Italian cuisine. Everything I liked to cook or eat seemed to have eggs in it, even salad dressing.

After our first year of marriage, when Marc and I were just starting to find our balance, his family emigrated from Lebanon. His eldest sister with her three-year-old nephew came first, then his sixty-five-year-old veiled mother, who didn't speak a word of English, with his youngest sister and brother-in-law and their daughter and newborn son in tow. Before I knew it, we were all living together in our two-bedroom, two-bath flat in San Francisco. All nine of us—six adults and three children under the age of five—packed into our spare bedroom and living room! From the fold-out futons to the portable crib, beds, pillows, and blankets took up every foot of our usable space, covering up my lovely accessories and French décor!

It wasn't just the lack of space and privacy that got to me, it was feeling that my words and actions were being examined and the overwhelming feeling of being a stranger in my own home. My world had turned upside down. I had gone from the West Coast to the Middle East overnight!

My small Country French kitchen soon became filled with hanging bags of yogurt dripping over the sink, buckets filled with live eels, and pots filled with raw cow tongues. It was the first time I had ever seen one, and trust me, it does not stimulate your appetite. Bags and bags of pita bread, huge jars of oils, olives, beans, dried fish, pickled eggs and pig's feet, and dried herbs filled my kitchen counters and fridge. My French baguettes and *Cooking with Julia* were replaced by pita bread and *Cooking with Aladdin*!

Dinner was a two-hour ordeal filled with ten or more plates of exotic foods and Arak, a one-hundred-proof liquor—exactly what my husband did not need! Between the Arabic music, food and language, I literally felt like a stranger in a strange land.

Marc and his family had no idea how hurtful it was to sit at my dining room table in my home and in the country where I was raised and not understand a word of what they said. I felt like a second-class citizen. When I confronted Marc about it, he told me I could like it or leave it, only very loudly in four-letter words! I found out fast where I rated on the family totem pole.

Although his family was kind, I felt lonely and disconnected from them and my husband, and so I did everything I could to occupy myself away from home, becoming a Jane Fonda exercise junkie and spending more time with my family in the suburbs. We lived like this for almost two months until, one by one, Marc's relatives found places to rent.

After they moved out, life returned to our version of "normal." The clubbing and night life I used to love seemed so empty and boring now–same people with new partners and the same stories, dressed up in new designer outfits.

I was bored. I wanted to find a job I could sink my teeth into. With my modeling and fashion background, I decided to try my hand working for a Greek designer we partied with. He imported all his clothing from Greece. He had boutiques all over the city and needed help in his corporate office. I heard he was a shrewd businessman, so I went for the challenge. After about eight months, I grew tired of the abusive hours, the disrespect he displayed to his employees, and the lecherous way he treated the young models working in his boutiques. Although he was never disrespectful to me, I kept a healthy distance from him.

At twenty-six, I found my life nothing like I had imagined it would be. I felt disconnected from myself and the hopes and dreams of my youth, and I had almost let the passion die that had fueled me since I was a child: making and baking cookies. Marc was allergic to eggs, and I didn't find pleasure in baking for myself, so I hadn't baked my delicious cookies and desserts that had brought me so much joy in years. Something had to change. Fate soon showed me what.

One day as I was walking along Chestnut Street about to begin a shopping spree, I began to smell a delicious aroma of freshly baked cookies. Following my nose, I continued walking down the street and then stopped in front of something I couldn't believe—a red-and-white cookie store called Mrs. Feels. I noticed a *help wanted* sign as I entered the store. Looking around, I stood there feeling my passion had materialized right in front of me. I was so excited that I went straight home without even shopping (a major sacrifice) and told Marc I wanted to start my own cookie business. Marc was a born entrepreneur and salesman, so having our own business appealed to him. He advised me to work at the cookie store, and if I still felt passionate about the business, he would support me. I did just that, and after two weeks of working part-time, I was offered the position of store manager. I declined their offer since I knew I wanted to open my own store, and I began spending every hour of every day on my lifelong cookie passion.

WHEN GOD CALLS YOU TO DO SOMETHING, HE ENABLES YOU TO DO IT.
—ROBERT SCHULLER[6]

While Marc traveled on business, I spent months researching the differences among commercial ovens, mixers, and refrigerators at restaurant supply stores; pricing equipment and ingredients; and meeting with distributors, packaging manufactures while experimenting with my recipes.

Obsessed with converting my small original recipes into large commercial-sized batches, I covered my kitchen counters with ingredients: bags of bleached, unbleached, pastry, and all-purpose flour; beet, cane, brown, and white sugars; salted and unsalted butter; Madagascar vanillas; rich gourmet chocolates; and fresh nutmeats. After many weeks of mixing, measuring, and creating batch after batch of cookie dough in my small San Francisco kitchen, breaking three hand mixers in the process, I perfected my recipe.

To test my recipes more thoroughly, I purchased a professional thirty-quart mixer and small convection oven, which I had delivered to my parent's large kitchen in the suburbs. For the next few months, my family, friends, and neighbors became our taste testers, comparing different chocolates, butters, nuts, and flavorings until everyone declared my cookies, "Perfect!"

Marc became involved, and he helped in developing the name Blue Chip Cookies. Mom and I created a stock market logo and packaging representing the best and highest-value cookie available to humankind! We fashioned a stock market uniform with Brooks Brothers white button-down shirts, blue neckties, jean skirts, and heeled shoes. And with the best cookies on the planet, we were almost ready for business. I continued searching for the perfect location for our first store and finally found one near Fisherman's Wharf across from the cable car turnaround, two stores down from the famous Buena Vista Cafe.

My husband negotiated the lease, and my parents loaned us their savings of fifty thousand dollars to begin building the interior of our first store. With the knowledge my dad had from building two family homes, he was able to design our store and work with the contractors to build our counters and install our commercial ovens, stainless steel sinks, metro shelving, and awning out front.

Two weeks before we were scheduled to open, my dad and Marc painted our store a stark white with a royal blue trim. Watching Marc teetering on the ladder in his designer jeans and tasseled shoes with a paintbrush in one hand and cigarette dangling from his mouth was a sight to behold. My mom and I spent countless hours putting Blue Chip stickers on thousands of white bags (we couldn't afford printed). The finishing touch was the blue-and-white tile mosaic of the Blue Chip stock logo in the front of our cookie counter, which became our trademark.

Most of the time I did most of the legwork and research, and Marc showed up to do the negotiating. Having a young wife with lots of energy was paying off! I thought he was supposed to take care of me, but as it turned out my passion was going to take care of both of us! Nine months and ten pounds later, we were finally ready for business.

At twenty-seven years old, I had unstoppable discipline and passion. After one week of operating our first store, and working consecutive sixteen-hour days, my mom and I traded our heels for athletic shoes and baggy jeans. We craved comfort, not cute! From day one, our cookies were in huge demand; lines snaked out the door, and we could hardly keep up. We busily mixed dough for White Chocolate Macadamia, Triple Chocolate, Black and White (created specially for San Francisco's Black and White Ball), Brickle Pecan, German Chocolate, Almond Toffee Chip, and Cappuccino—and of course the best chocolate chip, oatmeal raisin, peanut butter, and snickerdoodle cookies anywhere. All were served in the store on silver platters, and packaged in classic blue, white, and silver boxes and bags.

Pilots, businessmen and women, tourists, and celebrities lined up for my cookies. From Diane Feinstein to Clint Eastwood, my Blue Chip Cookies were becoming quite the culinary sensation among both the well-heeled and plebian. My cookies, totally unique and unquestionably gourmet, brought me the intoxicating aroma of success I had been yearning for.

My husband's skills as a born salesman combined with my creativity and gourmet cookies turned my passion into a very successful business.

Our most famous cookie was the White Chocolate Macadamia. In 1983, no one else had added white chocolate to cookies. To do this, we had to hand-cut ribbons of white chocolate into chunks because there was no such thing as a white chocolate chip. We spent hours tediously chopping three-, four-, and five-inch ribbons of white chocolate with a large French knife, always wishing for an easier way. Thankfully, my clever Uncle Bud, who had his own saw-sharpening business, created a manual cutting device for us that allowed us to cut many ribbons of white chocolate into hundreds of chip-sized pieces in a matter of minutes.

Our demand for white chocolate became so overwhelming that my grandmother Nana, who was wheelchair bound, volunteered to cut the chocolate for us using this manual device. She was so excited to be involved in our sweet enterprise. Nana understood the exhilaration of business ownership. Many years before, she had owned a small restaurant. It was there that she had become known for her mouthwatering chocolate chip and apple pancakes along with her apple, berry, banana, and coconut cream pies. Everything was created from scratch with lots of butter, sugar, and cream folded together with oodles of love, of course! As a young girl, I remember sitting at the counter and eating three kinds of pie with mounds of whipped cream until I was sick. My family's entrepreneurial spirit and love of sweets is in my DNA. I get a sugar high as visions of pies dance in my head.

My brother, Richard, got into the business too. He delivered clean aprons and towels my parents laundered at their home and the giant buckets of white chocolate Nana cut for us. We would quickly unload the chocolate, throw an apron on him, and put him to work scooping and baking the cookie dough as fast as he could while I continued mixing hundreds of batches. Making dough from scratch, lifting twenty- and fifty-pound bags of flour, sugar, and chocolate, and maneuvering the thirty-gallon egg buckets in and out of the fridge was hard physical work. With two hours for prep time, we were open by eight and closed by ten on weeknights and eleven during tourist season. Though I was always exhausted at the end of the day, the cleaning czar in me took over, and I would scrub the store from top to bottom until it sparkled.

I loved it when I could work with Richard. He had a way of taking any situation and making it funny, and I loved escaping from my reality with laughter. Some customers would come in asking if our cookies were made with blue chips, and he would tell them with a very serious face, "Actually they all start out blue, but the baking changes their color, and if you look very carefully . . ."

Struggling to keep a straight face, I would explain the definition of "blue chip" while ringing them up. Once they left the store, we laughed hysterically. As customers came and went, Richard would crack me up by imitating their accents and mannerisms. Many times it took everything I had in me not to lose it with a customer standing there.

We were all proud watching our cookie dough turn into spendable dough day after day, sometimes as much as thirty-five hundred dollars in one business day. At a dollar per cookie, that's a lot of dough!

Within our first year we had won several local and regional contests, and we were named by the *Oakland Tribune* and *San Francisco Chronicle* as the best new culinary sensation. *The San Francisco Bay Guardian* gave us the "Best Cookie in San Francisco and the Bay Area" award, stating our cookies were the "perfect combination of sweetness making your teeth tingle." *Inc.* magazine wrote, "nothing finer has passed my lips…may be the best cookie ever made." I appeared on several TV and radio talk shows promoting our Blue Chip Cookie company. We created quite a stir in the cookie business, considering we only had one store. Franchisees, shopping mall tycoons, and customers across the country wanted Blue Chip Cookies. We began shipping our cookies around the country. People were calling Blue Chip Cookies the "best cookies in the country;" some went as far to say best cookies in the cosmos!

Our demand for white chocolate chips inspired our chocolate supplier, Guittard Chocolate, to create a white chocolate chip just for Blue Chip Cookies. This enabled us to retire Nana and our white chocolate cutting machine.

My desire for cookies and the good life had led me down a very rewarding path. But much more than the material benefits, there was a deeper, more fulfilling reward. Doing something I loved and reaping the fruits of my labor made going to work exciting. I looked forward to it, and I started each day with boundless enthusiasm and pride. These were some of the happiest and sweetest days of my life because I was following my personal passion.

One of our Blue Chip stores

Mom and me opening day

LIFE INGREDIENT: PASSION
PASSIONATE WHITE CHOCOLATE CHIP

¾ cup butter, cold
¾ cup brown sugar, packed firmly
¾ cup granulated sugar
2 large eggs
2 teaspoons vanilla
2½ cups all-purpose flour
½ teaspoon salt

1 teaspoon baking soda
2 cups white chocolate chips or chunks*
¼ cup finely chopped coconut (optional)
½ cup macadamia nuts or pecans (optional)

➤ Preheat oven to 350 degrees.

➤ Line cookie sheet with parchment paper.

➤ In a large bowl, cream butter and sugars together; add eggs and vanilla, combining well.

➤ In medium bowl, using a dry measuring cup, measure out flour and level off excess with a knife. Add salt and soda to flour and mix well.

➤ Add flour mixture to butter mixture slowly, until just combined.

➤ Add chips, pecans, and coconut; stir until just incorporated.

➤ Using ice cream-type scoop, scoop dough into approximately 1½-inch balls. Place 2 inches apart and bake at 350 degrees for 14-17 minutes or until edges are lightly browned.

May substitute chocolate chips for white chocolate.

Makes 3 dozen cookies, depending on scoop size. Enjoy!

CHAPTER

3

Life Ingredient

FAITH

WHEN LIFE HANDS YOU LEMONS, MAKE LEMON BARS!

Faith moves mountains, but you have to keep pushing while you are praying.

—*Mason Cooley*[8]

There are times when our faith requires us to believe the impossible, to release that which we cannot control or guarantee and to walk down a path that is uncertain. When the answers we desperately seek are elusive, it is our faith which carries us through, bringing us back to the hope living inside each of us.

One of my favorite sayings (I guess it should be, because I made it up) is, "When life hands you lemons, make lemon bars." It perfectly illustrates how important it is to believe that obstacles—even huge ones—can become our opportunities if you continue to have faith in yourself and faith in God.

Within weeks of opening the doors of Blue Chip Cookies of San Francisco in March of 1983, Marc and I felt like we were on top of the world. But by September of that same year, the first sign of trouble in paradise began emerging, and my faith was seriously put to the test.

Six months into our business, we were slapped with a lawsuit alleging I had stolen "Mrs. Feels" recipes during my two weeks of part-time employment. "If that were true, then how many other hundreds of employees also had these recipes?" I asked our lawyer. This famous cookie company had been in business for five years and had opened more than fifty stores. We had just opened our first store. To me, the verdict was in: my cookies were the best! Why else would they go after us?

Although I knew I had done nothing wrong, I had never felt so scared and worried in my life. Instead of spending time running my business, I spent my days proving my innocence. The joy from our cookie store was mixed with bittersweet worry that that this lawsuit could put us out of business from the legal fees alone. My fears soon eclipsed the thrill of our financially productive days. Remembering the story of David and Goliath, I trusted in God and my faith to get us through this lawsuit.

This cookie giant had hired one of the largest law firms in San Francisco in an attempt to bury our Blue Chip name in expensive litigation. Their attorneys sent a deposition to some of our employees, my parents, my husband, and me. Feeling intimated as I walked into the huge conference room overlooking the city, I found myself with four slick, salivating lawyers sitting across from me, cutting apart my every word, sifting out any crumbs they could use against me and my company. This was an all-out cookie war, but I knew the ingredients of truth and faith were on my side!

To help prove our innocence, I brought home dozens of cookies from bakeries and cookie stores throughout the city, including Tom's, City Sweets, The Ultimate Cookie, Otis Spunkmeyer, and Just Desserts. I delivered them to the chemist we hired to be analyzed and compared to the Blue Chip recipe and Mrs. Feels cookies. After many elaborate and expensive tests, the chemist determined that our Blue Chip recipe was not like any others. This was the final evidence needed to slay this cookie monster. Thank you, God.

In the end, the victory was bittersweet, because the lawsuit cost us twenty-five thousand dollars just to prove our innocence, which was half of what we had invested to start our company. The Mrs. Feels cookie corporation failed to prove any of their fallacious allegations, and both our companies went back to business as usual.

I went back to making my gourmet cookies, and we opened a second, third, and fourth store. I was amazed how well Marc promoted and sold our cookies and company to shopping mall tycoons and franchisees without even having tasted what he was selling! Because of his egg allergy, he had never even taken one bite of my rich, sweet cookies. (I was later to realize there was much more of my sweetness he could never appreciate.)

My parents became full-time partners in the business, and Marc assumed the day-to-day financial responsibilities of the company as CEO. Because of an insatiable demand for my White Chocolate Macadamia Cookie, Guittard Chocolate Company continued making white chocolate chips for us, later making the white chips available to the entire baking industry. Meanwhile, my Blue Chip Cookies became known as, "The Best Cookies in the Country (BCC)" and

Take the first step in faith. You don't have to see the whole staircase, just take the first step.

—Martin Luther King, Jr.[9]

continued to receive awards and win cookie contests and shopping mall contracts throughout the country. With our thirteen (baker's dozen) gourmet varieties baked daily from scratch and my commitment to maintaining the highest standards, I assumed we were on our way to a most satisfying future! *Assumed* was the wrong word. Never assume anything!

As it turns out, the cookie business wasn't as sweet as I thought. We waged bitter battles, which grew to feel more like a bitter war. With my cookies constantly upstaging the largest player in the industry, it became a money and real estate game of bidding wars for the best locations, publicity, and promotions. The cookie rival was continually making it more and more difficult to succeed. They had deep pockets, venture capital, and many store locations; we lacked the financial resources needed to fight the cookie war. The demands of expanding our company robbed us of what little pleasure we could glean from a seven-day work week and long hours away from home. I couldn't work enough to satiate the gluttonous appetite of the business, and at a dollar per cookie, it took a lot of dough just to pay the rent, which was upward of three thousand dollars per month at some locations.

And although our Blue Chip stores were successful, my fairytale marriage was turning into a war of wills. Well, what could I expect when I had married a man sixteen years my elder, raised with a different religion and culture? A man who was allergic to eggs and unable to sample, much less appreciate, one of my best talents?

Because both of us shared the bond of love for our families, many gatherings would start out enjoyable but ended up with Marc's getting drunk. When I would confront him about his drinking, he would retaliate by yelling and name-calling. The more I stood up to him, the worse it got. With no one but me willing to tell him the truth about his alcohol addiction, the lies continued, as did the drinking. It's no wonder our fiery romance turned into a raging firestorm!

Blue Chip Cookies and my faith in God seemed to be the only things holding our marriage together. Like the binding quality of eggs in cookie dough, my faith and beliefs are what kept me in my marriage. That same faith also kept me in this abusive relationship because I thought I was unable to leave what God had joined together.

I was not a quitter. I felt the obligation to finish what I started; besides, what would happen to Blue Chip and everything I had built? Plus, now both our families were involved in the business, which added to the pressure to keep it all together. Still I stayed, feeling responsible for all our family members and their livelihoods, especially my parents, who were our business partners. By breaking up my marriage, I would destroy the image of the company, damage its profits and new franchisees, and lose the cookie war. And did I mention the financial pressures of a personal guarantee Marc and I had signed for a million dollar bank loan from Merrill Lynch to expand our company?

I did not want to burden my parents, so I went to a pastor I knew for marital advice. When I shared with him about Marc's binge drinking, name-calling, pushing, and shoving which sometimes caused bruising, the minister did not seem overly alarmed. His only comment was, "Do you feel safe?" I told him that I supposed so, not knowing how I really felt. Like so many women living with emotional and physical abuse, I was both confused and scared. The minister went on to tell me how a godly wife could win her husband over, which I interpreted to mean my actions could control Marc's drinking and tyrannical behavior. Here I was finally asking for help and protection, and instead I walked out of this man's office feeling misunderstood, powerless, and trapped...in the name of God.

I believed that adding one more ingredient would help hold our marriage together: children. After two years of trying to get pregnant and one miscarriage, I finally became pregnant, and I was very excited. I persuaded Marc that moving out of the city would help our faltering marriage, and we would be in the best place to start our family. Looking back, I realize I was dealing with everything but the real problem.

I found a sixty-five-year-old, three-story Country French home in the hills of Piedmont with panoramic views of Marc's favorite things, San Francisco and the Golden Gate Bridge. Piedmont, a wealthy suburb, instantly spoke of prestige and the sweet life, and I knew Marc would relish that. I did the legwork and found the house, and Marc negotiated and closed the deal.

After the birth of our first daughter, Adele (whom Marc named after his deceased mother who had lived with us), I thought things would change and become more normal and happy. We had it all: a beautiful daughter, a gorgeous home, and a sweet business which was growing more successful every day. And the icing on the cake was that soon I became pregnant again, nine months later delivering another beautiful baby girl named Lindsay after a famous actress I admired.

Marc adored his daughters and spent every moment he could with them, and he even became more moderate with his drinking when he was around them, giving me renewed hope. We looked like the perfect family and picture of success on our custom Christmas cards—a dark, exotic father, a blonde model mother, and daughters who matched each of us.

To celebrate a banner year at our stores and our nationwide shipping business, Marc and I hosted a beautiful Christmas party at our home for our managers, friends, and family. The white lights twinkled on our elaborately decorated floor-to-ceiling Christmas trees and fresh garlands. The Poinsettias and gourmet fare were abundant. Except for our bartender dressed as Santa (who drank more than he served), everyone agreed it was a fabulous Blue Chip party.

Though we looked perfect from the outside, our marriage was unbearable at times. We kept it together at work, but once we got home and the girls were in bed, Marc would pour himself a tall scotch and start complaining about business: financing new stores, frequent employee thefts, increased rents, and rising ingredient costs, all the while pouring more scotch to numb the stress he was feeling. When I pointed out to him how the drinking was not helping the situation, he'd blow up at me with more name-calling and physical threats, telling me I was the cause of his pain. For the longest time, I lied to myself about his alcoholism and abusiveness because I was worried about tainting my (and our company's) image.

Those times when Marc couldn't drag himself out of bed after a bender, I lied for him and told the office staff he was sick. I had worked so hard to create my heart-shaped cookie-cutter life, and I was doing everything I could to keep it all from crumbling. So I told myself that if I loved him more and worked even harder, things would improve, just as the minister had advised. For too long I focused on fixing Marc instead of fixing myself.

One evening while Marc was drinking heavily, I was upstairs lying on the chaise in our master bedroom, reading my Bible and praying. As I opened my Bible to an unfamiliar chapter from the Old Testament, a scripture verse was illuminated and jumped off the page, compelling me to read it.

It read, "For I know the thoughts and plans I have for you,' declares the Lord. 'Plans to prosper you and not to harm you, plans to give you hope and a future."

I felt that God was speaking directly to me. I closed my eyes to begin meditating on the verse, feeling peace and comfort. Suddenly Marc flung the door open and stormed in. Charging over to me, he grabbed my Bible out of my hands and threw it out the open window three stories down into our terraced garden. This book, so holy to me, had landed somewhere on the ground between the fountain and beds of French tulips below. Without a word, Marc stormed back out of the room. I broke down and cried my heart out to God.

NOW FAITH IS BEING SURE OF WHAT WE HOPE FOR AND CERTAIN OF WHAT WE DO NOT SEE.

—HEBREWS 11:1 NIV[10]

Though Marc had tried to control everything in my life, even my spiritual beliefs, miraculously my Bible survived without even a tear in the pages. However, my heart felt torn to bits. If not for the love I gave and received from my daughters, Adele and Lindsay, my heart would have fallen apart completely.

My girls brought me so much joy during those tough times, especially on Sunday mornings, when the San Francisco 49ers football game played early. Marc loved watching the game at home without distractions, so it was a perfect time for the girls and me to practice our faith. I would take Adele and Lindsay to Sunday school with me while I attended the church service. The girls loved the Bible stories and songs they learned, happily singing them while driving to and from church.

One Sunday after the girls and I got home, Marc took Adele and Lindsay to The Piedmont Market for groceries. They loved shopping with him and riding in the cart together, knowing their dad would always buy them a treat. He thrilled in doing so as much as they loved it. But this day, when he came home from shopping he walked into the kitchen fuming. "What's happened, Marc?" I asked. "What's wrong?"

"Your daughters were singing 'Jesus Loves Me' the entire time I was shopping," he said with a snarl, "and I've never been more embarrassed."

Laughingly I asked, "Is that why you're so upset?"

"Stop brainwashing my daughters!" he screamed, dumping the bags of groceries on the counter and storming out as I stood trembling with Adele and Lindsay by my side.

Later that day, Marc stretched out on the sofa to watch the reruns of the game. Adele and Lindsay climbed onto his stomach. Lindsay started singing a Bible song. Adele scolded her with, "Daddy doesn't like Bible songs."

"Does Daddy like Jesus?" Lindsay asked her older sister.

Adele turned and looked directly at her father with her dark brown eyes and chocolate-colored curls and asked Marc, "Daddy, do you like Jesus?"

Quietly and reluctantly, without taking his eyes off the game he said, "Yes, I like Jesus." He probably thought that would satisfy her, and he turned up the volume to make sure of it.

But Lindsay, hearing his reply, swung her blonde curly locks and big blue eyes about two inches from his face and looked him squarely in the eyes. Boldly she asked, "Daddy, would you like to serve him?"

Marc was speechless, and I burst into laughter and couldn't stop. Angrily glaring at me with dark, piercing eyes, he ordered the girls to go play while he cranked up the volume of the game so loud I had to leave the room.

Leaving Marc was on my mind constantly those days. I found the courage to file for a separation three different times, spending thousands of dollars retaining lawyers. Each time Marc found out, he would threaten to fight me for custody of Adele and Lindsay and leave me penniless. So I would back down from fear feeling overwhelming defeat. *What's wrong with me that I cannot find the strength to follow through?* I began reading books about alcoholism and codependency and soon discovered that my life was a textbook example of both. Living with Marc was like riding a roller coaster with Dr. Jekyll and Mr. Hyde; I never knew which one would show up. He was tyrannical and unpredictable.

When he was Dr. Jekyll, he apologized with flowers or jewelry, explaining how stress from the business, employees, and family made him drink too much. Hoping to undo the damage from the night before, he'd promise to curtail his drinking and never yell at me again. But soon Mr. Hyde showed up again, and he was impossible. I avoided him like the plague but still suffered panic attacks that I sought to assuage by taking long walks or hot baths.

I was deeply worried about how a divorce might damage five-year-old Adele and three-and-a half-year-old Lindsay. Yet their behaviors were revealing that they felt the effects of our loveless marriage. When they heard us argue, they often cried and ran to me, wanting me to hold them. Once when Marc called me repeatedly a f------b----- after I poured out all his Black Label scotch and hundred-year-old cognac, the girls were within an earshot. Adele started crying. It broke my heart and hurt them terribly to see their daddy screaming obscenities at me. The next morning after Marc had left for the office, I went upstairs

Fear ends where Faith Begins.

—UNKNOWN

into our bedroom to make the bed and found Adele in her daddy's walk-in closet pulling down the last of his designer ties from his tie holder. There lay thousands of dollars worth of ties on the closet floor. She said she didn't know why she did it, but I certainly did. Of course I hung them all back up, like a good codependent. And Lindsay, who had heard the abuse since she was in my womb, would cringe and run to my side when she heard Marc raise his voice in anger. I kept on trying to save the marriage, remembering the minister's words.

During this time, my parents and family knew of some of the abuse, and they recognized the severe drinking problem Marc never acknowledged. However, they still left it up to me to solve the problem. I grew up believing divorce was unacceptable, unimaginable, and unforgivable and didn't feel strong enough to make such a huge, life-changing decision that affected so many people I loved. No one around me had encouraged me to leave my marriage, not even my pastor, so I took that as an unspoken directive to stick with it. Entrenched in denial and codependency, I allowed my fears instead of my faith to control me. Over and over, Marc threatened that he would leave me penniless and fight me to his death if I divorced him.

Yet all the while I wondered: *Where did my voice go? What happened to my dream of living happily after?* This wasn't turning out the way I thought. My rich, exciting, and luminous life had lost its luster.

There were many, many dark days. But my faith in God was my constant light throughout. Ironically, it was my faith that kept me going, but that same faith also kept me from leaving. My belief and hope that things could and would get better kept me going until I finally reached a point where the pain of staying exceeded the fear of leaving.

The straw that broke the proverbial Middle Eastern camel's back came the morning after an evening of intense arguing, followed by a terrifying dream. It was about eleven at night, and Marc was very inebriated. As I got ready for bed, he followed me into the bedroom and bathroom trying to provoke me by calling me names such as, "controlling bitch" and, "pathetic mother." There was something evil-sounding in his voice, and he glared at me almost with hatred. My gut told me to leave, but I did not think I could since my daughters, Adele and Lindsay, were asleep in the next room.

Marc stumbled out of our bedroom and held the hand rail tightly as he went downstairs for another drink. I could hear him bellowing out loud to himself, growing more belligerent every moment. I heard him on the phone yelling at someone in Arabic for the next twenty minutes and then slamming down the phone. I felt drawn to my daughters and quietly tiptoed into the bedroom they shared. I kissed Lindsay, who was curled up in her crib, and slipped into Adele's twin bed, which I had never done before. I lay next to her, as still as possible.

"Please God don't let Marc come in here," I prayed. "Let my daughters sleep peacefully." I pleaded. "Please protect them from Marc's rage."

I don't remember falling asleep, but I do remember a vision as real and detailed as it was terrifying. As I lay there, eyes closed and praying, I saw hundreds of black, terrifying, winged gargoyle-like creatures filling the hallway and flying wildly against the door of Adele and Lindsay's room, trying to get in. The only thing keeping them out was the door, or maybe my prayers. This vision or dream seemed to go on all night as I cuddled next to Adele. Eventually I fell into a restless sleep.

The next morning, remembering the night of visions more terrifying than any horror movie I had ever seen, I wondered: *Was that dream revealed to me from God?* Had I conjured it up from my own conflict and pain?

The house was deathly quiet, and I was anxious and nervous to see what might be lurking behind the door, or downstairs in the living room.

Slipping quietly out of Adele's bed, I slowly opened the door and saw that everything in the hallway looked normal and untouched. The frames hung level on the wall. The door was solid and smooth, but it looked like a hurricane had struck downstairs. I tiptoed into the kitchen and found burnt cigarettes teetering on the window ledge, broken shards of glass from brandy snifters on the kitchen floor, and the phone dangling from wall. When I walked into the living room, I found Marc passed out and snoring like a goose on the sofa. He looked old, weak, and so sad that I actually felt sorry for him. At that moment, I realized I no longer feared him or his threats. My faith in a kind and just God helped me summon the strength to break through the fears that had immobilized me. My worries, my feelings of responsibility for others, my vanity, and my need for security vanished that morning.

WHEN LIFE HANDS YOU LEMONS, MAKE LEMON BARS.
—LORI NADER GRAY

I hurriedly threw a few outfits for my daughters and me into my Louis Vuitton duffel bag. I awakened Adele and Lindsay and together we tiptoed out the back door, my precious sleepy-eyed girls in their PJs and me in my sweats, careful not to wake the sleeping lion.

Driving to my parents' house, I had a firm sense that nothing mattered as much as my peace of mind and my daughters' well-being and safety. I felt happier than I had in a decade. I knew my girls and I needed and deserved a whole and healthy family, and I didn't want my marriage to forever tarnish Adele's and Lindsay's perceptions of love and marriage.

In what felt like an instant, the multimillion-dollar business, the three-story French Country home, the Jaguar, and the nanny disappeared. In their place was a single mother driving a used Toyota and living in a small home in the suburbs with her two young daughters. The fairytale marriage and the entire picture-perfect story collapsed like the house of cards it was.

But what remained throughout was my faith in God, which was what ultimately led me to rediscover and give power to the belief that I deserved better. And by empowering myself through books on codependency and alcoholism, prayer and faith, I was able to leave my abusive marriage. I realized the security that I had clung to for so long was not nearly as valuable as the priceless feeling of taking those first steps towards a happier future that was truly sweet and not artificially sweetened.

Creating at the mixing bowl

My cookie monsters—
Adele and Lindsay

Love at first bite

LIFE INGREDIENT: FAITH
FAITH-FILLED LEMON BARS

For the Crust:
½ cup softened butter
¼ cup granulated sugar
1 cup all-purpose flour
For the Filling:
3 large eggs at room temperature
1½ cups granulated sugar
1 tablespoon grated lemon zest
½ cup freshly squeezed lemon juice
½ cup all-purpose flour
confectioner's sugar for dusting after cooling
parchment paper to line the bottom of baking pan

➤ Preheat oven to 350 degrees.

➤ Line an 8 x 8 inch baking pan with foil or parchment paper with excess hanging over sides.

➤ **For the crust:** Using an electric mixer, cream butter and sugar until light and fluffy. Add the flour to the butter mixture and mix until it holds together. Press the dough into baking pan, building up a ½-inch edge on all sides. Chill.

➤ Bake the crust for 20-25 minutes, until lightly browned. Let cool on wire rack for 30 minutes.

➤ **For the filling:** Whisk together the eggs, sugar, lemon zest, lemon juice, and flour. Pour over the cooled crust and bake again for 30-35 minutes, until the filling is set. Let cool.

➤ Cut into squares and then dust with powdered sugar.

Makes 16 large squares. Enjoy!

CHAPTER

4

Life Ingredient

FORGIVENESS

THE KEY TO BEING FREE!

Anger makes you smaller, while forgiveness forces you to grow beyond what you were.

—*Cherie Carter-Scott*[11]

Finding forgiveness is like turning the key and unlocking the door to contentment. Anger and resentment are a ball and chain that will keep you locked up behind lonely walls inside your soul. If you want to live a fulfilled life, you must open that door. Peace has a price, and that price is forgiveness.

I'm not sure which came first, the chicken or the egg. But forgiving others and forgiving yourself go hand in hand, that much I know for sure. Forgiveness is the key to being free–free from feeling like a victim, free from soul-poisoning bitterness and anger, free from turmoil and frustration, free to live a balanced, delicious, and happy life!

70

After Marc and I divorced, I shed my designer jeans and shoes and traded my Estee Lauder for Maybelline. With the exception of an occasional panic attack, I was beginning to feel good about myself. My life was simple. I lived near my parents and sister Debbie, who both supported me emotionally. Although I had walked away from my passion and the company I created, I knew with utter certainty that I had done the right thing in saving myself and my daughters by walking away from the trappings of success.

Adele and Lindsay visited their father in San Francisco every other weekend. Marc signed up to get help for his alcoholism. It was the only way the court would allow him to see his daughters, whom he loved and missed dearly.

On those long weekends when Adele and Lindsay were with their dad, I was able to spend considerable time with me, myself, and I. But who was this trio? I hadn't the slightest idea. Piece by piece, I started putting my life back together. Outwardly, I was in my prime, thirty-five years old, strong and fit from my work-outs at home with Jane Fonda and *Buns of Steel*. But inside I felt wounded, fragile, and scared.

For more than a year I started seeing a wonderful counselor every week without fail, whether I felt I needed it or not. Many times I would walk in feeling I didn't have an issue in the world to talk about and then leave in tears, mascara running down my face and arms filled with more books and tapes to learn from. At times I hated spending my limited alimony on counseling. Counseling was something that no one could see, and I thought it would have felt much more enjoyable to buy tangible items like clothes or shoes. But I was willing to submit to "psyche surgery" in order to understand what had made me marry and then stay in such an abusive relationship. Thankfully, my insurance picked up half my counselor's fee, but even so, it just killed me to go window shopping, knowing there were fabulous half-price handbags with my name on them that I could not afford.

To forgive is the highest, most beautiful form of love. In return, you will receive untold peace and happiness.

—Robert Muller[12]

Marc had bought my share of the company for pennies on the dollar, and the child support was intended for my children, not for me. I had to find a job. I decided to take more control of my life and go back to school to get my teaching credential. Halfway through the teaching program, I realized I did not want to be around children all day and then come home to more children who were so much more important to me and who needed me so badly. I began to acknowledge the voice inside telling me that I did not have the patience or passion for that! Another year went by, and I still didn't know what I wanted to do.

I knew I loved houses, decorating, and helping people, so I changed course and went to school for my real estate license. After dropping off the girls at school, I would head to Anthony's Real

Estate School and learn about townships, easements, land rights, and all the legalities of representing buyers and sellers. (Real estate classes were as boring and tasteless as the coffee from the vending machine outside the classroom, and if it weren't for the M&Ms I munched while taking copious notes, I never would have gotten through the classes.) After completing real estate school, I began studying for my state exam at night after I had put the girls to bed. This was serious stuff, and it took countless hours and numerous bags of plain and peanut M&Ms to memorize all the tax formulas and real estate definitions I would never use. Thankfully, I passed the exam and joined the Walnut Creek Mason McDuffie Brokerage firm, and within three months I had gotten my first listing!

After less than a year in real estate, I realized my favorite part of my work was getting a home ready for sale—painting, decluttering, and decorating—and I had become so good at it that other agents were asking me to help them with their listings. I *finally* knew what I wanted to do. Shedding my business suits and heels and donning my jeans and tennis shoes and carrying a toolbox, I started my own home-staging company, Home MakeOvers. The best part of the job was that I could work while Adele and Lindsay were at school. No more nights and weekends showing properties and holding open houses. Of course, the money didn't compare with what I could earn in real estate, but I was no longer letting money sway my decisions. I was listening to the voice inside and trusting my instincts.

As for my internal rebuilding, I began attending church more, and I started writing in a journal. The more time I spent reflecting, the more I realized how many years I had harbored resentment towards Marc and how my resentment was imprisoning me. Even though we had been divorced for several years, I still felt controlled by Marc. He withheld the money he owed me from the buyout of Blue Chip Cookies and at times even child support. We fought about money constantly, hiring lawyers numerous times just to enforce our divorce decree. I had heard a quote somewhere that, "He who has the gold has the power," and I felt powerless. The pennies on the dollar that I had retained from the multimillion-dollar company that I founded, sweat, cried over, and ultimately left behind was barely enough for us to live on, and the money would eventually run out.

It was hard to believe Marc did not have abundant funds from which to provide more support and remuneration to me since every time he drove up in the latest Jaguar, he was wearing Armani

FORGIVENESS IS THE
KEY TO BEING FREE.

—LORI NADER GRAY

suits and Gucci shoes, telling me that "his" company (Blue Chip Cookies) was losing money, and he could not afford to pay me what he owed. It was a cash business, which meant he controlled the books and cash flow. As he constantly cried poor to me, I cried my eyes out to God, praying that He free me from this man and his manipulation. I truly felt my life would be better if Marc ceased to exist. Ours was a classic love-hate relationship. I loved what we had built together and the way he loved our daughters and my daughters loved him, but I hated his anger, his arrogance, and mostly his manipulations.

I had divorced him to get away from his control, and yet I still felt imprisoned by Marc. By the same token I allowed him to have power over me by grasping for the money he owed me— money he dangled before me like a diamond Tiffany necklace just beyond my reach.

Praying fervently to God, I begged for help with my hateful feelings and for freedom from my worries. Yet I still clung to those, feeling as if I were engaged in a bizarre game of tug-of-war. After many years of battling and stirring it up with Marc, God impressed upon me that He could not answer my prayers if I did not let go. Soon, I would have to let go. But not in any way I could have possibly imagined.

It happened one night when Adele and Lindsay were in San Francisco spending the night at their dad's house, and I was alone for the weekend. Marc came to pick them up, conveniently forgetting to bring me my check as he had so many times before. As he drove off in his silver Jaguar XJS, anger, frustration, and hate boiled in my soul like a bitter brew in a witch's cauldron. I went to bed, crying and entreating God to intervene in my life. I remember questioning Him out loud. "Why haven't you helped me? When are you going to do something, God? I can't keep fighting this man and this battle!"

I remember as if it were yesterday how He answered me. Although I didn't hear Him audibly, I saw the answer in writing on a ticker tape inside my head. It read, "I've been waiting for you to be ready." The words penetrated my heart, and I broke down into tears. I had been impeding my own growth and healing. When I was ready, healing would happen and my circumstances would improve. I realized I needed to forgive Marc and let go of my bitterness. I drifted off into a peaceful sleep, forgetting to set my alarm, and was jarred awake by a harsh ringing. I fumbled to find the phone, only to feel it freeze in my hand as I heard my daughter Adele's panicked cry.

"Daddy's fallen in the shower, and his head is bleeding! Help us, Mommy!"

I immediately hung up and called 911 to send an ambulance to Marc's Pacific Heights flat. Calling Adele back, I asked her if I could speak to her dad. *Is he awake?*

She handed the phone to Marc, and in a terribly weak voice, he told me the pain was unbearable. "It feels like knives are splitting my head open and I don't think I'm going to make it." He continued in a barely audible whisper, "Tell the girls how much I love them. I'm sorry for hurting you and driving you away."

"Marc, hold on please. Don't let go. The ambulance is on its way." I pleaded with him and with God.

His feeble voice continued, "You need to know there is a bank account at B of A with your name on it, and all the money I owe you is there."

Feeling overcome by love, in tears I begged, "Please hang on, Marc! You're going to make it!"

It was unbelievable that this was happening and at this time. Both Marc's married sisters, one of their husbands, and their children who all lived in San Francisco had gone to Lebanon for a visit. As soon as I hung up with Marc, I called the remaining brother-in-law at work to drop everything and asked him to please pick up Adele and Lindsay from Marc's and drop them at their summer camp to wait for me because I was on my way into the city to pick them up. Next, I called my parents and asked them to meet me at the hospital. Speeding over the Bay Bridge, my mind was filled with disbelief and shock as I thought about what had happened in the past twenty-four hours. Worries about Adele and Lindsay and what they had witnessed that morning flooded my mind and made me tremble more than I had when I feared Marc would strike me.

When I picked the girls up from camp, I hugged them tightly. The three of us rode in silence to the hospital. When we arrived, the doctor pulled me aside and told me in a hushed, matter-of-fact voice that a massive brain aneurism had ended Marc's life in the ambulance on the way to the hospital. His heart was still beating, but his brain was dead.

I felt outside of space and time. Not one family member was around, just ten-year-old Lindsay, twelve-year-old Adele, and me. Sadly, that night Marc's heart stopped before his family could arrive home from Lebanon, and I had to sign the papers to release his body to the morgue. Crying over his lifeless body, my daughters and I said our last goodbyes. He was fifty-six years old. About a year later, Blue Chip Cookies was sold to the highest bidder, and I never walked into another Blue Chip store or tasted a Blue Chip cookie again.

Reflecting on what had transpired those last few hours, I realized that Marc's telling me about my bank account was his way of making peace with me before he passed. He had forgiven me, as I had forgiven him.

His death, with the turmoil leading up to it and what Marc had said while he was dying, was a powerful lesson in forgiveness. I realized how much time we had lost being angry at each other. I finally forgave Marc for his abusiveness under the influence of alcohol. With a compassionate heart instead of an embittered one, I accepted the fact that Marc had been an addict, and when he wasn't drinking, he was a loving, kind, and generous man whom I had once loved. He was a loving father who had helped me realize my dream of having children and a partner who had helped me fulfill my passion of starting my own cookie business.

I had let myself feel victimized for far too long, and I had blamed Marc for destroying Blue Chip Cookies. I blamed my parents for not protecting me from his abusiveness. But I especially blamed myself for having failed and for not living up to my own expectations. How crazy was that? Here I had been a successful model, created profitable businesses, birthed two beautiful daughters, won writing contests and modeling contracts, and earned a Bachelor of Arts degree from UCLA. Yet I still felt like a failure for what I hadn't done "right."

Learning to forgive myself and accept the fact that I was not perfect—and did not have to be—was the hardest lesson. I realized things were beyond my control, including Marc's death. I did not cause it, nor could I have prevented it. With so much out of my hands, that's all I could really ask of myself.

There was no manual for how to live life, and I had done the best I could with the tools and knowledge I had at the time, and only after forgiving others could I forgive myself.

LIFE INGREDIENT: FORGIVENESS
SWEET FORGIVENESS SUGAR COOKIES

½ cup butter, softened
1 cup granulated sugar
1 large egg
½ teaspoon vanilla

2 cups all-purpose flour
2 teaspoons baking powder
½ teaspoon salt

> Combine flour, baking powder and salt in bowl.
> Beat butter, sugar, egg, and vanilla at medium-high speed in mixer bowl until smooth.
> Add flour, gradually mixing at low speed until just blended.
> Gather dough into a ball; divide into 2 disks.
> Wrap and refrigerate 4 hours until firm or overnight.
> Preheat oven to 350 degrees.
> Grease 2 large cookie sheets or line with parchment paper.
> On a lightly floured surface (may use confectioner's sugar or flour to flour surface) with floured rolling pin, roll one disk ¼-inch thick. Cut out desired shapes with 4-inch or 1¾-inch miniature cookie cutters.
> Transfer to prepared cookie sheets and keep at least 1 inch between cookies.
> May decorate at this point with colored sugars and candies, or leave plain for icing later.
> Bake 7 to 10 minutes until edges begin to turn golden.
> Transfer cookies to wire racks to cool. Repeat rolling and cutting remaining dough, re-rolling scraps.
> Decorate as desired with icing of choice.

Makes approximately 2 dozen cookies. Enjoy!

THE CHIP THAT NEVER BLENDED IN!

Courage is resistance to fear, mastery of fear—not absence of fear.

—Mark Twain [13]

Only after the sting of twenty-twenty hindsight do we usually acknowledge that we chose the wrong path, because we didn't feel confident enough to trust our instincts and God in the first place. Ultimately, happiness or unhappiness is our own responsibility. Blaming others or a situation, or making excuses won't get us off the hook. Finding courage to trust your inner voice may mean having the strength to release yourself from the golden handcuffs of a job you despise, breaking off a relation-

ship with the guy who is perfect on paper, or changing a deeply ingrained habit.

Only when you have the courage to honor your feelings will you be prepared to act in your own best interest and stay on course. Many people like to think they know what is in our best interest, and attempt to win us over to their point of view. But there is no one better equipped or better informed to do best by you than you. So why not listen to yourself?

I had only been divorced a year when one of my girlfriends invited me out to the single scene, and we ended up at Tommy T's comedy club. We were laughing at the comedians and enjoying a glass of wine when a guy named Chip came over to me. I hardly noticed him until I heard a voice that reminded me of the Disney character Goofy asking, "Gosh, what's a nice girl like you doing in a place like this?" His voice cracked me up. Though I wasn't attracted to this goofy guy, I politely made small talk. I was still unsure of myself and a little embarrassed to be a divorced mom out in the single scene. Even though I felt stronger physically, being a single parent of two young daughters while trying to make a living was wearing me down emotionally. I still believed in marriage and partnership. So once again, I began dreaming about finding someone to take care of me, even though I was doing a pretty good job of it on my own. I just didn't see it that way.

Chip continued entertaining me with his character impressions, and I continued laughing. It did feel good to be out and to have someone pay attention to me.

Chip said he was a lawyer but had aspirations to be the next Jay Leno, so he was there to check out the comedians and learn new material. He was so different from other men I had dated and was the complete opposite of Marc in every way. Physically, he was fair-skinned with thick, stick-straight sandy hair that he parted way over on the left side, and he was about my height. He wore a short-sleeved shirt, flood-length khakis, shoes that tied, and I thought I even spied a pocket protector in his pocket. He was anything but Metrosexual!

Chip told me he was British, although he was the complete opposite of the sexy Winston Man from my past. I was used to exotic, tanned, handsome, mysterious, and sexy men, and Chip was an average, ordinary-looking guy who didn't stand out in a crowd. But there was something about him that felt very safe, and I did enjoy his dry, sarcastic humor and intelligence. I learned he was politically conservative, agnostic, and had a doctorate degree. He didn't drink much, had never tried drugs, and hated smoking. I learned quite a bit about him in that one night.

TRUST THE AUTHORITY OF YOUR SENSES.
—THOMAS AQUINAS[14]

But even with so many positive attributes, there was something inside telling me Chip and I weren't a match. When he told me he was a single dad and had a son named Derek who was the same age as my daughter Lindsay, I started rationalizing. *Physical looks are so overrated and superficial. Your whole life has been about image, and where did that get you? Lori, give the guy a chance. You can always give him a makeover and take him to church!*

So I gave Chip my phone number, and he began calling me every night after my daughters went to bed. He was so easy to talk to and soon we were talking for two and three hours each night about our pasts, our hopes and dreams, and even sexual fantasies. I didn't realize how vulnerable and needy I was at the time. I was in my sexual prime (mid-thirties) and hadn't been touched physically or felt loved or appreciated in years. Chip's flattering words and attention night after night were seductive. His soothing, deep voice reciting the poetry he wrote took me to another place, making me forget that he had a "face for radio," as he called it.

After so many night chats, I finally agreed to a date with Chip, and within three weeks we had become intimate. It was the first time in years I felt truly loved, appreciated, and finally safe enough to let someone into my heart. Chip's adoration for me became a healing balm to the wounded soul I carried from my abusive marriage to Marc.

Chip paid attention to my every word, at times taking notes on the three-by-five cards he carried with him. He thought my every word was important and my stories so funny that he even had me laughing about them! He was forever in search of the next great line or joke...but he was also forever in search for the perfect job. His passion was to become a famous comedian or comedic writer, but at forty-three, he was not willing to move to L.A., live in his car, or wait tables. Chip idolized Jay Leno, and after we had been dating for about a year, he surprised me with a trip to Lake Tahoe and backstage passes to Leno's show. Meeting Jay Leno only added fuel to Chip's smoldering desire to become a famous comedian.

Chip's dissatisfaction with his life and the full-time law career he walked away from worked as a temporary solution for me. With his knowledge of the law and extra time on his hands, Chip became indispensible to me helping me file the right papers to fight legal and child support issues with Marc's trust. It was such a comfort to have a lawyer on my side for a change, saving me thousands of dollars in legal fees.

Chip was a brilliant lawyer and occasionally accepted part-time work in law in order to make ends meet, but he resented every minute of it. His dream was to become famous at the microphone telling jokes and entertaining the audience. When he worked at his passion of writing comedy he was happy and content, but he was still unemployed. This was a continuing problem for us as a couple.

Chip was not only a skilled lawyer, but he also had tremendous talent for impersonating famous rock and roll singers, which paid well. Occasionally he would be hired to perform for parties and black-tie events, and I would come along for support. We would arrive early to set up and stayed long after the party was over to tear down and pack up all the sound equipment. While Chip entertained everyone singing his favorite rock and roll songs, I mingled solo in the crowd with other attendees dressed to the nines. I enjoyed rubbing elbows with wealthy doctors, lawyers, and businessmen and women while sipping wine and checking out auction items I couldn't fathom having the money to bid on.

Many times, I would be approached by eligible bachelors who asked if I was single or who I was with. Flattered and somewhat embarrassed, I would answer, "I'm with the band" while sometimes thinking *the hired help*.

I loved Chip's passion for music and comedy, and it never would have been an issue for me if he would have kept his day job in law. I understood the importance of working in your passion, but the reality of mortgage payments, health insurance, utility bills, food, clothing, and automobile expenses were ongoing.

I went along with the program for some time, especially when I saw how Derek, Adele, and Lindsay got along famously. I thought our lives could eventually blend together and hoped that Chip would bond with my daughters. But Chip did not know how to be playful and connect with them. He even refused to sing or play his guitar for us at home. That part of him was reserved only for the stage.

> WE GAIN STRENGTH, AND COURAGE, AND CONFIDENCE BY EACH EXPERIENCE IN WHICH WE REALLY STOP TO LOOK FEAR IN THE FACE . . . WE MUST DO THAT WHICH WE THINK WE CANNOT.
> —ELEANOR ROOSEVELT[15]

Chip's idea of showing the children love was to correct their manners, grammar, and homework and teach them math games or send them outside to play so he could have me all to myself. All my daughters wanted was acceptance, unconditional love, and fun like they had with their dad. Chip was not that person.

Although he was helpful and attentive, which I sorely needed at the time, we were still two puzzle pieces that just didn't quite fit. I gave up wearing my heels so I wouldn't tower over him. He didn't attend church with me; socially, he was an introvert while I have always been a classic extrovert. Chip saw the world as problematic, with the glass half empty, while I optimistically saw the world overflowing with possibilities. Chip's legal mind saw the minefield in everything and he even carried a chip on his shoulder most of the time.

I'll never forget the trip we took to Hawaii to celebrate the three-year anniversary of our first date. Chip sat on the beach under an umbrella wearing a white undershirt and white socks, trying not to get his pale white skin sunburned. While we observed other couples parasailing or riding jet skis, he declared, "Those sports are too risky. They're a lawsuit waiting to happen." And here I had been thinking suntans, swimming, and adventures! How vividly our stark differences stood out to me at that moment. Even to this day I can recall all that whiteness with such clarity, I almost needed to reach for sunglasses!

You might think I would have realized that it shouldn't take a couple of glasses of wine at the beginning of our "date nights" for Chip to become more attractive to me. Instead of picking up on that clue, however, I tried with all my might to convince Chip to work full-time, change his religious views, and get him to exercise, care about his appearance, and stop being so negative. And no matter how hard I tried, I just couldn't silence that nagging voice inside: *You are not where you need to be, he's not the right fit for you.* So round and round I went in a state of self-induced angst, exhausting myself while attempting to make the relationship work and make Chip what I wanted, needed, and deserved.

But my fears of being alone and insecurity about what others thought after almost four years together (plus a huge dose of self-criticism) all kept me captive, and my insecurities about his finances began wearing on me and our relationship. This waffling went on for seven years. We dated, became engaged, broke up, and became reengaged. While Chip was searching for that "perfect" job, I became the perfect codependent cheerleader, a job description I knew too well and fell right back into. After all, he was working hard at getting a job in his "passion," which I understood and hoped would lead us to a sweet and successful life. And Chip's love for me was helping my heart to heal and making me stronger. I was determined to be there for him to help him become successful.

I second-guessed my feelings of discontent and frustration, telling myself maybe I was expecting too much. I knew Chip loved me; he showed me that love through handmade cards, love letters, and foot rubs, which helped me feel emotionally connected to him. And I finally felt safe, knowing Chip would never abuse me or leave me. Even though he managed to make enough money to pay his mortgage without full-time employment, I never felt totally secure. After such a tragic and tumultuous first marriage, my dream was to create a safe and loving family for my daughters and me.

So after investing seven years in our relationship, when Chip finally landed full-time employment performing law seminars, I agreed to marry him. From the fire into frying pan! Deluding myself into thinking Chip's lack of employment had been our only problem, I soon realized nothing had changed...except my name.

We both sold our small homes and combined our finances to find a larger home for our blended family and Chip's home office. After Chip added eleven addendums to the real estate contract (of course), we agreed on the terms and bought our *Brady Bunch* house.

Our financial security lasted about two years, until Chip's company no longer needed his services full-time. I continued staging homes while he went back to dreaming, writing, and hoping it would lead to success. With his part-time work and my income, we managed to pay our household expenses.

Not having the courage to listen to the voice inside screaming at me when I first met Chip–that same voice I managed to turn down to a whisper years later—lead to three years of marriage counseling, blended family counseling, and far too much arguing between us and our kids.

We argued about everything big and small, but especially our children. "We can't afford it," "Money doesn't grow on trees," and, "Keep the kids quiet" became daily phrases and were echoes of ghosts from my past. Instead of facing the heart of the matter, which was my own dissatisfaction in the relationship, I dealt with my frustrated feelings by attempting to control my life in external ways such as throwing myself into painting and redecorating our house or planning a budget vacation we could afford. I forever tried to create the picture-perfect family outings which never quite turned out like the brochures.

I became the social and cruise director, household manager, children's caretaker, and heart and soul of our home. Coming home exhausted and physically beaten after staging houses all day, I hoped Chip, who worked at home, would surprise me with dinner prepared. A roasted chicken from Costco would have thrilled me at this point. But to my continued disappointment, the house would be dark: no music, no savory dinner aroma, no table set, no nothing. Instead I would find Chip in his office, working at finding his next job or writing comedy, buried in paperwork and oblivious to time or the life going on all around him.

Without my energy, verve, and sparkle, our home felt dead. Soon I began to feel dead inside; my heart and soul became buried in conflict and pain. Not so much for me, but for Adele and Lindsay, who never felt a loving connection to Chip. What I had been looking for was a soul mate and partner as well as a loving father for my young daughters.

My hope was to create a home where our children felt comfortable, laughing and playing with their friends in our beautiful backyard pool setting. Instead, Chip wanted our home silent as he worked from his home office, deep in thought and paperwork. "Children should be seen and not heard" was not the way I wanted to raise my daughters! And finally when I brought home a giant trampoline for our pubescent, energetic kids, he adamantly refused to put it together and wanted a "hold harmless" signed before any of their friends could jump on it. Our *Brady Bunch* life was not turning out the way I had envisioned. Chip made excuses why he was unable to attend the girls' soccer games or occasionally pick our kids up from school when it was a scorching one hundred ten degrees. "They can tough it out and walk home, like you and I had to," he would say sarcastically. And because Chip did not desire to connect with them in the way they needed, the girls essentially remained fatherless.

With Chip, everything was calculated by the cost plus the benefit and then divided by the worst-case scenario. I would tell him passionately "Chip, I appreciate having you as an anchor in my life, but an anchor has got to be pulled up if we're ever going to sail to other shores!"

Feeling like a rat on a treadmill, I continued trying to create the life I dreamt of through external means by keeping things going. But no matter how beautiful the decorating or how exciting the Costco cruise sounded, ultimately they proved unsatisfying and bland. It was like having a cold—my taste buds couldn't taste the true flavor of anything.

My partner and I weren't connected in a way that we could appreciate our joint endeavors, and our arguing was eroding what intimacy we had. One beautiful sunny morning after carpooling kids to school, I came back home feeling down and totally defeated. I had completely run out of energy. Feeling depressed, I kicked off my sandals and crawled back into bed fully dressed. A hopelessness came over me, and I stayed in bed for half the day as Chip worked in his home office.

Chip was oblivious to the damage and scars caused from his negativity, and the need for my constant arbitration as the referee in our family had finally worn me out. It was on that morning I realized the cost of staying married became greater than the benefit of moving on.

It wasn't one specific big thing that brought me to the breaking point, it was so many things. I couldn't take it or fake it anymore. I accepted the truth that had always been in my heart, and finally had the courage to act on it. We were never meant to be marriage partners—my "ah-ha" moment, ten years in the making.

Better late than never, I suppose, but what a huge waste of a decade. I could have saved my daughters and myself a lot of grief had I just heeded my instincts from the beginning.

I grew up and grew stronger from our relationship, which I will forever be grateful for. But if I could do it over again, I would hope to have the courage to trust God, myself, and my feelings, because not doing so just delayed the inevitable.

All that was accomplished by staying in the relationship was that it was extended into a ten-year journey when it should have been left at my door at the end of our first date. The outcome was the same in the end. Staying on this misguided path exhausted much of my energy and in turn negatively affected my daughters.

Too often, however, it seemed easier to pull the covers over my head and go back to sleep, drowning out the voices with sounds of shopping malls or loud music, and staying asleep at the wheel. Instead of waking up, I threw all my waking energy into trying to change the situation or person in order to create the outcome I was seeking, distracting myself from the truth.

A decade had passed since I had met Chip. I was forty-four years old, and after being married for three wearisome years to him, I had mustered the courage to face my fears and accepted that I needed to change course and separate from him.

But accepting this was only the first step. Next I had to find a way to actually do it, and I had no idea how I would. I didn't know how I could possibly start over and set up a new home for Adele and Lindsay without completely disrupting all of our lives. Putting a "For Sale" sign in our front yard and uprooting his son and my daughters was not what I wanted to do, but I didn't have the financial resources to set up a new, independent household. Everything I had was invested in our big *Brady Bunch* home. There were no easy choices. A sense of hopelessness played into the very fears I was trying to overcome. I started second guessing my feelings and praying to God for answers.

Backstage with Jay Leno

LIFE INGREDIENT: COURAGE
COURAGEOUS OUTRAGEOUS OATMEAL

½ cup butter, softened
½ cup peanut butter
½ cup brown sugar
½ cup granulated sugar
1 large egg
1 teaspoon vanilla
¼ cup Karo (light corn syrup)
¼ cup wheat germ (or may substitute ground flax seed for gluten free)
½ teaspoon salt
½ teaspoon baking soda

½ cup flour
2 cups oats (quick)
¾ cup shredded coconut
½ cup chocolate chips or butterscotch chips
1 cup plain or peanut M&Ms(optional)
½ cup white or dark raisins (optional)
½ cup sunflower seeds (optional)

➤ Preheat oven to 350 degrees.

➤ Line cookie sheet with parchment paper.

➤ In a large mixing bowl, blend sugars well at medium speed. Add the butter and peanut butter, mixing to form a smooth paste. Then add Karo. Add egg and vanilla to butter mixture, blending until light and fluffy.

➤ Add the flour, salt, baking soda, oats, and wheat germ. Stir until just blended. May need to use a large spoon.

➤ Stir in remaining ingredients until mixed evenly. Dough will be very thick.

➤ Using a regular ice cream scoop, scoop dough onto the lined baking sheet about 2 inches apart. Press down slightly and bake for 16-18 minutes. Remove to cooling rack.

Makes approximately 3 dozen, depending on size of scoop. These are really fun cookies to make and eat—so get the kids involved and enjoy!

THE MIRACLE MONEY!

Nothing can be done without hope and confidence.
—*Helen Keller*[17]

Where hope grows, miracles blossom.
—*Elna Rae*[18]

Hope is a powerful leavening of life. It is a belief in a positive outcome. Hope allows us to wish for something with expectation or confidence with the feeling that what we want can be had, or that events will turn out for the best. It's the thought that there is something bigger, something truer, something totally surprising out there waiting for us.

Hope is composed of equal parts courage, work, will, and faith: giving us a passion for the possible, believing tomorrow could be better than today, that you will get a second chance, that you can make a difference, and that you matter.

Embrace the power of hope; it always swirls all around you. It will transform your life, strengthen your heart, and lift your spirit.

I told Chip and our marriage counselor that I wanted a separation and break from our marriage since nothing was working, including Chip. Although Chip was very upset about my desire to separate, he wasn't upset enough to make any changes. He was unwilling to go back into full-time law, and he continued to blame Adele and Lindsay for our problems.

Neither one of us could afford to live elsewhere, so we endured living together while we created separate lives. Chip's negativity was as thick as my dad's special two-flavor fudge. He became hunched over and moped around the house growling, "Your daughters got what they wanted. They won!" How sick is that? No one had won. We all were losing. My hope for our *Brady Bunch* life was dead, and it saddened me to see Adele, Lindsay, and Derek lose their hope, too.

For the next six months, I prayed for a way out.

And then it came— the "Miracle Money." I call it that because out of the blue, a simple phone call opened the door to my future. Again my prayers were answered in a way I could have never imagined.

My oldest daughter, Adele, had just turned sixteen. Because she had passed her driver's test, I called the trustee of Marc's estate to see if any funds were available to help buy her a car. Thankfully there were, which meant no more borrowing of my car.

After resolving the car issue with the trustee, I was about to hang up when he casually mentioned that he had made a note to call me that week about another matter. He said an oil company Marc and I had bought stock in during our marriage had been sold, and they were liquidating all the shares and distributing the proceeds to the owners. They found Marc's trust, which would help with Adele and Lindsay's college fund, but since I was the co-owner, they needed to send me my proceeds as well.

FOR I KNOW THE THOUGHTS AND PLANS THAT I HAVE FOR YOU, DECLARES THE LORD, PLANS TO PROSPER YOU AND NOT HARM YOU, PLANS TO GIVE YOU HOPE AND A FUTURE.
—JEREMIAH 29:11

I had completely forgotten about our community property stocks and never expected to hear the trustee's next words: "Your shares are just over one hundred thousand dollars. Where would you like me to send the check?"

The amount of money at the time was staggering. And it just happened to be enough for the down payment on a house!

Immediately, I began looking at available homes on the market, but after two months I started to give up hope because I couldn't find anything in my price range. The Bay Area is ridiculously expensive, and a half-million bucks buys very little here (though we do have million-dollar weather to compensate for it).

I actually did find two houses that I could afford, but both sold before I could put in an offer. So the following Saturday, I drove to my agent's house and asked for a list of every house on the market in my daughters' school district, even ones over my price range.

I noticed one house that had been on the market for almost six months and was out of my reach financially, but because it was on Hope Lane, I felt compelled to see this house. For some reason, it represented the hope I was desperately hanging on to. My agent wasn't available that day, so I decided to check out the house by myself. While driving there, a beautiful song was playing on a CD I had purchased nine months earlier. It was by a Christian artist who had played at my church. The song I was listening to was entitled, "A Vision of Hope."

As I pulled into the cracked driveway, it looked like the house had been vacant for a while. It quickly became obvious that my "vision of hope" needed much renovating and a lot of TLC. I pushed open the broken gate and walked into the park-like back yard with its overgrown liquid amber trees, evergreens, weeds, and ferns. Giant pink camellias, white hydrangeas, and lilies surrounded the old rickety deck, and a large Japanese maple next to the back sliding door added both brilliant color and serenity to the scene. I felt a sense of peace I hadn't felt in years.

I was dying to see the inside and started checking the doors to see if I could get in. The rusty bedroom sliding door was unlocked so I walked in. It was a classic 1970s rancher, a well-laid-out single-story, four-bedroom, two-bath home that needed more work on the inside than it did out. Green shag carpeted the floors throughout; smoky crackled glass and brass ball light fixtures hung from chains in the kitchen and bathrooms. Foil wallpaper and matching drapes beautified one of the bedrooms, while bamboo cloth and floor-to-ceiling brown paneling adorned the others. The linoleum was peeling from the kitchen floor, and even the bathroom ceilings were wallpapered. But despite needing a new driveway and new windows, floors, wall coverings, light fixtures, landscaping, fencing, cabinets, and appliances, it was absolutely perfect!

I knew it was the house in which Adele, Lindsay, and I were meant to start our lives over and get back on the path we were intended to walk as a family. Though it was way over my price range, I had faith that somehow God would make it happen. With tears in my eyes, listening to "A Vision of Hope," I hurried home to get Adele and Lindsay. They were still in their pajamas when I breathlessly exclaimed, "I found our house!" They were excited about our moving out as long as they didn't have to change schools. "Jump in the car, girls, and I'll show it to you, and then we'll drive through McDonald's for breakfast!" As we drove past the fire station and a tranquil park and duck pond, I told them how perfect the house was and that they could pick out their rooms once we got there. I hoped in my heart it was the vision of hope house for us!

As we pulled into the driveway, the girls sounded disappointed as they made sarcastic comments about the ugly chipped paint, rusty windows, and overgrown weeds in the front yard. They hesitantly got out of the car and I led them into the backyard. They liked the overgrown flowers and trees and immediately decided a hot tub would make it "totally" perfect! I pushed open the rusty back sliding glass door, and we all entered the house as if it were a sanctuary. After a couple minutes of silence, both my loving, kind, and hormonal middle and high school daughters blurted out, "This house is gross, Mom! We can't live here! This carpet is sick!" Ignoring them, I continued walking through room after room like a game show hostess, pointing out the features of each room and changes I would make. I wanted them to visualize "our" house with the wallpaper, paneling, and carpet removed and new light fixtures and cabinetry. They had seen me work my magic on houses before. I knew how to strip wallpaper and faux paint and use a power drill and screwdriver. And what I couldn't do on my own, I would find a way to accomplish.

THERE IS NO MEDICINE LIKE HOPE, NO INCENTIVE SO GREAT, AND NO TONIC SO POWERFUL AS EXPECTATION OF SOMETHING BETTER TOMORROW.

—ORISON SWETT MARDEN[19]

The girls both finally agreed with all my ideas. "It could become a nice house," they admitted as they reluctantly picked out their rooms, talking about the silver color Adele wanted for her modern chrome furnishings and the tan colors Lindsay wanted for her leopard theme.

As we drove away from the house on Hope Lane that morning, I felt happier and more hopeful than I could remember. My agent immediately presented an offer way below asking price, and after intense negotiating (a skill I had learned from Marc), the sellers accepted my offer.

I staged our failed *Brady Bunch* home and put it on the market. While waiting for it to sell and for Hope Lane to close escrow, we continued to live with Chip and Derek. Although it wasn't comfortable, living at Hope Lane in its current condition would have been far less comfortable. So we endured. Chip and I avoided each other as much as possible. He still accused me of betraying him and was convinced my daughters were victorious, and he was the victim. His reality of the situation just confirmed my conviction that his negativity controlled him, and I needed to get out.

Hope Lane closed escrow on December 23, 2001, and by the twenty-sixth I had torn out the kitchen and relocated the cabinets to the laundry room. I worked on the house daily and hired a contractor friend I knew from my staging business, paying him time and materials to help me realize my "vision of hope." With a Home Depot credit line, I started remodeling immediately. I knew I could repay the loan once I got my half of the proceeds out of our *Brady Bunch* house.

Those days were challenging (filled with hard work—emotionally and physically). Before the girls went to school, with my cup of java in hand, I started my day working on our Hope house or buying materials for the contractor at Home Depot. Then I ran off to my staging jobs and back to Hope after dinner, working until late in the evening. For three months I stripped wallpaper, sanded and painted the old woodwork, and pulled hundreds of carpet tacks and staples out of the floor after pulling up the worn shaggy carpet. I was cleaning and weeding like my old days; the house shaped up, and so did I. Even my skinny jeans were hanging off me. I've found there's nothing like a divorce or remodeling a house to drop some extra pounds!

The girls and I moved in by the middle of March. We threw our first party celebrating "Best Picture" with the Oscars on TV, and our "Best House" and my miraculous makeover. It was the first of many happy and joyful parties at Hope Lane.

Ironically, shortly after we had moved into Hope Lane, without her even knowing my new address, my niece gave me a book she had brought home from a women's conference. She said she just felt it was something I needed. The book was called *The Allure of Hope* by Jan Meyers. Remembering the scripture that had popped off the page of my Bible almost twenty years ago reconfirmed my belief that God was telling me to walk toward my destiny with faith, courage, and hope. All these outward signs of hope were giving me the thumbs-up that moving to Hope Lane had been the right decision, reinforcing the idea that "when one door closes, another opens."

LIFE INGREDIENT: HOPE
HOPE-FILLED DREAMS

¾ cup confectioner's sugar
1 cup butter not softened
2 cups all-purpose flour
1cup finely chopped pecans or
  walnuts
1-2 Tablespoons cold water

1 teaspoon vanilla extract
½ teaspoon almond extract
¼ teaspoon salt
extra powdered sugar for
dredging

➤ Preheat oven to 350 degrees.

➤ Line cookie sheets with parchment paper.

➤ In a mixing bowl, cream together the butter and sugar, then add 1 tablespoon of water, flavoring extracts, and 1 cup flour with salt. Repeat with remaining flour, nuts, and water*.

➤ *May not need 2 full tablespoons water, add just enough water until mixture holds together in a ball.

➤ Use a small scoop or roll dough into a 1-inch ball. Place on an ungreased or lined cookie sheet.

➤ Bake for 15 minutes until the bottoms are lightly browned.

➤ Remove from cookie sheet and let them cool on rack.

➤ Once cool, roll in powdered sugar until well coated.

Enjoy!

CHAPTER 7
Life Ingredient
HUMOR

CHAMPAGNE THERAPY!

*I think the next best thing to solving a
problem is finding some humor in it.*
—Frank Howard Clark[20]

Surrounding myself with people who make me laugh and looking for the humor in situations has helped me cope with much of the pain and heartache over the years. Humor and sadness run parallel in all of our lives. Laughter is healing and helps us move on in life instead of staying mired in pain and becoming bitter. I find laughter releases the toxins from my soul and lifts my spirit, and I have always felt a great release after a good belly laugh with friends or family.

It has always been my choice to stay positive and in finding the humor in my situation. I eventually find the lesson, too.

After we moved to Hope Lane, I found two bulky packages as I was weeding through my closets— the wedding dresses I had stored for years from my past marriages. The dresses were so different from one another, just like my marriages had been. My first nuptial gown was unique and unconventional, with a sophisticated ballet-length imported lace skirt and matching bodice pulled together by a creamy satin sash. It had been ridiculously expensive.

My second bridal dress, purchased from a factory outlet, was from the Jessica McClintock collection: conservative, full-length raw silk with a princess neckline. Chip thought weddings were a waste of money. We argued about everything from costs to chair placement, so it's no wonder it rained on our parade, literally! The downpour on our wedding day had called for an ark!

What was I thinking? I had gone from one extreme relationship to another. My first husband was aloof and arrogant, rarely listening or paying attention to me. My second husband followed me around like a needy puppy, taking notes on three-by-five cards about my every word.

After my musings, I thought of my nieces, who were both in serious relationships. Surely one of them might want one of my beautiful designer wedding dresses. I picked up the phone on my nightstand and dialed one niece, then the other.

Each girl had the same response. "Thanks, but no thanks, Aunt Lori." They wanted to wear wedding dresses that represented a successful marriage, not jinx the most important event in their lives. I understood completely, and so I decided to take the gowns to a consignment shop and get some of my money back from them. The shop owners said they would happily take them off my hands if I would be willing to have the dresses freshly dry cleaned. After receiving a quote of over hundred dollars apiece to clean them, I lugged those gowns right back home and hung them up in my closet again.

A few weeks later, I received a notice that a Salvation Army truck would be in my neighborhood the following week for curbside donations. *Perfect.* So Tuesday morning I placed the old soccer shoes, rollerblades, and garden pots, along with my two designer wedding gowns, on the curbside in big black bags for pickup. After I twist-tied the bag closed, I began laughing at the irony of the situation. Something that once had tremendous value and deep meaning had been reduced to a trash bag. I called my friend Keri, whom I had known since high school, to share the story. She found the humor in everything, and I knew she would not judge me. I could hardly get the story out; we were both in tears from laughing so hard. It felt so good to release those sad memories of my life with tears of irony instead of tears of despair.

Laughter and tears are the best part of what my girlfriend Karyn calls, "champagne therapy." This is a time when four or five of my best girlfriends get together and share everything on our minds while we sip champagne and graze among some appetizers. Finally being old enough to appreciate our differences without jealousy, we share beauty secrets and talk about our children, our husbands, hormones, new recipes, and new boyfriends. Together we've been through divorce, remarriage, new careers, facelifts (not mine), births, the complexities of married life, and the struggles of being single. By openly sharing our lives, we gain insight and knowledge–and also a few extra pounds from the delicious hors d'oeuvres and cookies we munch throughout the evening! But it is completely worth it.

Champagne therapy dictates that each of us takes the podium one by one to share our latest stories or concerns and to receive sage advice or just to vent. (Heaven knows I've spent my share of time venting at the podium!) Before the night is over, we all laugh so hard our mascara runs down our faces, and we run to the bathroom to clean up before we go home.

Of course, what's said in champagne therapy stays in champagne therapy, and it's much more fun than a shrink!

But I have been given permission to share these stories: One summer evening outside in my peaceful back yard on Hope Lane (during champagne therapy) my friend Lisa told us about

RED FLAGS NEVER CHANGE THEIR COLOR.

—LORI NADER GRAY

Craig, a new guy she was dating. He was a pro football player who loved to dance and sing, and he loved dogs, especially his Rottweiler, Rombo.

"That's really a good sign," I told her. "Men who love dogs are usually more balanced and giving in a relationship." The girls all nodded in agreement.

"But every time we're together, Rombo is with us," she complained. " Rombo was there on my first date at the park and second date for lunch when we ate outside, and Craig even brought him out to dinner with us, leaving him out in his truck to drool all over our seats while we dined. He goes to work with Craig, sleeps with Craig, and even watches us during sex, then jumps up on the bed to sleep between us!"

We laughed hysterically as she continued. "Every day Craig cooks a special meal for Rombo, but he has never even so much as whipped up an omelet for me." After her rant, Lisa asked the group, "What should I do, girls?"

I could not stop myself from blurting out. "Run far, run fast! He's codependent with his dog! You'll be in third place every time and in the doghouse before long." They howled with laughter as I continued, "Don't forget what I've learned, Lisa: Red flags never change their color!"

Taking the podium next, Leslie told us about John, an extremely handsome guy she was dating, who had a great job in the wine business and dressed like a *GQ* model. Leslie said she was instantly attracted to him, but that there was just something about him that she couldn't put her finger on. Asked to describe him and her concerns, Leslie grimaced and began. "He highlights his hair more often than I do, spends time tanning more than I do, runs religiously every day, sometimes twice a day, is carb-a-phobic, and won't eat a tortilla chip with Mexican food or crackers with cheese; and he irons everything, including his underwear!"

My friends and I looked at each other with wry grins.

"He's more meticulous and fastidious than I am," Leslie added, "And you girls know how neurotic I can be!"

We all nodded in agreement, laughing and pouring more champagne.

"Every time I go to his house, he's still primping, which is starting to drive me crazy. Once he's finally ready, we do have a great time together, but I just don't know if I want to take this to the next level. I've never dated someone who takes longer to get ready than I do."

Jumping up to the podium, I confidently announced to the group, "I know what the problem is, Leslie!" All eyes looked my way, and the girls grew silent, "It's the HMx2 rule, and it'll never work."

Then Leslie asked seriously, "What is HMx2, Lori?"

"He's high maintenance, and you're high maintenance. There can only be one high maintenance person per relationship. HMx2 is a formula for disaster! Sorry girlfriend, but red flags . . ."

I didn't need to finish my sentence because the girls all chimed in. ". . . never change their colors!"

Later that evening, after a few glasses of champagne, my champagne therapy club talked me into doing something I never in my wildest dreams thought I would do—learn to scuba dive. My girlfriend Kim excitedly told me, "You'll have a blast, Lori. You'll meet adventurous new people, you'll challenge your mind and your body, and the best part is that most of the scuba masters are hunks!" Not giving me time to object, she continued. "You might finally meet a healthy, normal, down-to-earth guy who loves a little adventure!"

"But I'm claustrophobic, shark-a-phobic, and a recovering control freak," I insisted.

Ignoring me, Kim was rummaging through her purse. She handed me the scuba school's business card. "It'll be the most unique experience of your life, Lori, and it will help you overcome your phobias and break through your fears. Promise me you'll try it, Lori."

"I promise," I said, pouring myself an extra-full glass of champagne and wondering what in the world I had just gotten myself into.

A promise is a promise for me, so I signed up for scuba lessons the very next day. Within an hour, reality and anxiety kicked in, and I began slaying my "fear dragon" several times a day as I prepared myself for my underwater adventure. Recalling my days during my modeling career of swimming with the killer whales, I kept telling myself: *It will be a piece of cake, Lori, since there are no dragons underwater, just sharks!*

THE MOST WASTED OF ALL DAYS IS ONE WITHOUT LAUGHTER.

—E.E. CUMMINGS[21]

When I showed up for classes in my new bikini, my freshly highlighted hair hanging down over my shoulders, the "hunk" instructor barely looked at me as he introduced himself as Scottie. He tossed a hideous neon-green-and-orange wetsuit my way. "Here put this on," he demanded as he passed me a heavy black vest filled with weights, a yellow mask, and blue flippers. Nothing was color coordinated, and I felt both uncomfortable and physically unattractive, not to mention scared out of my mind.

After I struggled forever to get the wet suit on, Scottie looked at me disdainfully. "The zipper goes in the back, not the front." He sighed. No wonder I was so uncomfortable! I'm sure it had nothing to do with the weighted vest, tight face mask, snorkel, and extra-long plastic flippers.

I remained optimistic as I turned the suit outside in, hoping this experience would turn out well. Expecting to feel like Jacqueline Bisset from *The Deep*, instead I felt like Lucille Ball in one of her crazy *I Love Lucy* costumes. I awkwardly strutted over to the very handsome and tanned Scottie to confide my concerns about sharks, claustrophobia, and my control issues. He assured me he would keep me safe in the ocean, telling me that before I knew it, I would be as comfortable as a fish underwater. All I could think was that if God meant for me to swim like a fish, He would have given me gills.

Day after day, we met for classes at the pool. I became the perfect student. I paid strict attention to Scottie's instructions and every word—after all, my life was literally on the line. After spending hours together one on one, Scottie began warming up to me. I lingered around after class to help him put the equipment away and to begin my seduction...or so I thought. After all, he never talked about having a wife or a girlfriend, so that had to mean he was interested in me. I wasn't sure whether he was taken by my positive can-do attitude, my magnetic personality, or maybe my curves. Whatever it was, I liked what was happening, and I felt confident that Scottie liked me.

The day had finally come for my first open-water scuba adventure. I was ready to take the dive and conquer my fears, impressing Scottie with my sporty, playful personality.

As the boat slowed down in the middle of the ocean, I felt the need to remind Scottie of my concerns again, so I approached him coyly. Scottie beat me to the punch. Before I could say a word he said, "I know, Lori, you're claustrophobic, shark-a-phobic, and a recovering control freak. Now finish getting your gear on, we're just about at the reef."

As we slowly slipped into the ocean for my first dive, I asked Scottie not to take me down too deep. I told him I needed to know I could get to the ocean surface if I panicked. "To be out in the middle of the ocean, dependent on a tank and vest for my very survival, is a huge stretch for me, Scottie," I continued, hoping for some compassion.

He responded unsympathetically, "Lori, I know you can do this, now let's go!"

As we dove under the water together, I visualized our bodies synchronized like playful dolphins; I fantasized that I was a mermaid meant to seduce him. At the same time, I reassured myself that everything would be okay. I reminded myself: *Just don't forget to breathe: in and out, in and out.*

Following Scottie closely, I began to relax. Looking around, I saw schools of neon-yellow-and-orange fish, vibrant-colored coral, and sea urchins moving under the water. We had been underwater for about thirty-five minutes, and just as I started to feel truly comfortable, Scottie took out his underwater chalkboard and wrote, "U R at 75 ft."

My eyeballs bulged and the old claustrophobic, shark-a-phobic, control freak wanted to punch his lights out and bolt to the surface. But forcing a smile, I continued swimming a little faster and closer to Scottie, repeating to myself: *It's just a number, like your weight on a scale. You're okay, it's just a number, just keep breathing; in and out, in and out.*"

After my third and final dive that day, I was no closer to feeling like a mermaid, a dolphin, or a fish under-water. I happily climbed back onto the boat. Throwing off my gear, I tried to comb out my matted, tangled, salt-filled hair and let the creases from my face mask fade. Checking myself in my compact, I saw my waterproof mascara smeared around my reddened eyes and my all-day lipstick blotted around my mouthpiece. This was not a very glamorous sport. In fact, at that moment I realized it was not my sport at all.

A HAPPY HEART MAKES A CHEERFUL FACE.
—PROVERBS 15:13

I strolled over to Scottie in creases, tangles, and smeared makeup and thanked him for keeping me safe and for helping me overcome some of my fears of the deep. He gave me a high-five, picked me up and hugged me tightly, saying, "You did it, Lori! I'm so proud of you!"

Then Scottie asked if I'd like to join him for a celebratory beer on the boat with the captain, whom I had never seen or met. I excitedly said "Yes." I knew Scottie liked me. This could be the start of our romantic adventure together. He had answered my siren call!

After our boat pulled up to the dock, Scottie pulled out our beers just as the captain (who was even more buffed, tanned, and gorgeous) appeared on deck. As I sipped my beer, I thought, "Wow, if Scottie and I don't hit it off, I have a possible backup plan."

Just as I was savoring this fantasy, the captain walked over to Scottie and gave him a big hug and a gentle kiss on the lips. Scottie looked at me. "Lori I want you to meet my partner, Steven."

Choking on my beer, I struggled to say, "Nice to meet you."

I laughed to myself, almost out loud. I thought I was getting better at reading men. *The girls at champagne therapy will never believe this!*

It had never occurred to me that Scottie could be gay. *Was that chemistry I was feeling or too much carbon dioxide from my oxygen tank?* This had not turned out like a Danielle Steel romance novel–what a huge waste of my time and energy.

Standing up, I chugged my beer and said my goodbyes to Scottie and Steven, finally laughing out loud as I walked down the pier. "Maybe next time, I should take up sailing," I said aloud.

Live well, love much, and laugh often…life is too short to do anything else!

Making a splash

KEY INGREDIENT: HUMOR
LOL (LAUGH OUT LOUD) SNICKERDOODLES

½ cup buttercold
¾ cup granulated sugar
1 large egg
1½ cups all-purpose flour
1 teaspoon cream of tartar
1 teaspoon baking soda

¼ teaspoon salt
In a separate small bowl
combine:
¼ cup granulated sugar
1 teaspoon cinnamon

➤ Preheat oven to 350 degrees.

➤ Line cookie sheet with parchment paper.

➤ In mixing bowl, combine butter and sugar until all butter lumps are gone. Add egg and combine.

➤ In a separate bowl, combine flour, tartar, baking soda, and salt. Whisk together.

➤ Add to butter mixture and combine. Roll spoonfuls of dough into palm of hand and roll into balls the size of a walnut. Place on plate.

➤ In a small bowl combine the remaining sugar and cinnamon and mix.

➤ Roll dough balls in the sugar/cinnamon then set on cookie sheet about 2 inches apart. Bake for 12-16 minutes or until edges are slightly golden. Let cool and set up on cooling rack.

Enjoy!

CHAPTER
8
Life Ingredient
BALANCE

THE LONGER YOU'RE SINGLE, THE BIGGER YOUR COJONES!

A well-developed sense of humor is the pole that adds balance to your steps as you walk the tightrope of life.

—William Arthur Ward [22]

After almost a half-century, I have finally learned in order for me to change, my conversations must change. A fulfilling life is a balance of flavors, textures, and sweetness that are perfectly folded together and then baked to perfection. To get there takes years of subtracting, remeasuring, and substituting ingredients— then overbaking and underbaking until you get the balance just right. And by choosing differently, your behaviors will change. For this to happen, you have to BE different so you will DO things differently in order to HAVE a different outcome and ultimately a batch of wisdom worth sharing.

Achieving balance as a single parent—combination mother, father, nurturer, disciplinarian, social planner, homework cop, and career woman was overwhelming and impossible. After Marc died and my divorce from Chip, Adele and Lindsay wanted to be with me twenty-four-seven. Many times I would lose patience with them and feel guilty because I wanted just to escape from it all. Whatever I did never seemed like enough. I began comparing myself to other moms and families I encountered at school, the grocery store, and just about anywhere. I never measured up to them in my opinion.

I filled all those empty voids by becoming a "human doing," something I am very good at. My modeling and Blue Chip years had rewarded my perfectionism, and the payoff I experienced from the physical aspects of my life were always greater than the rewards of being vulnerable. I was running from my staging jobs to school, to swim meets, to soccer games, to planning birthday parties, to making dinner, to science projects, and to falling into bed exhausted—starting all over again the next day. If I ever see another extra-credit art project, I think I'll scream!

Unfortunately Adele and Lindsay learned the same behavior from me. My daughters picked up on the insecurities which materialized in my keeping a perfectly neat and decorated house, my obsession with my workouts, and my complaints of a few extra pounds. They started becoming more defiant and started gaining weight. I realized something was emotionally eating them up on the inside, but I didn't know how to help them.

I should have realized the balance I needed for myself and my daughters was a life filled with **less** and not **more** outside distractions and activities so that the three of us could learn to feel and stop avoiding the emptiness inside.

I knew the spiritual and emotional parts of me were still out of balance from the embarrassment and shame I felt about being divorced not once, but twice. And although I looked and acted strong on the outside, I was still fearful and insecure on the inside. Always afraid of looking out of control, I never let anyone—including my daughters—see me cry about anything. Anger and frustration were okay, but

THE LONGER YOU'RE SINGLE THE BIGGER YOUR COJONES.
—LORI NADER GRAY

not vulnerability or sadness. The distorted message I was telling myself and my daughters was that being vulnerable was a weakness. And as a single mom and career woman, I felt that I had to become even stronger and less vulnerable. Another one of my personal mottos has always been, "The longer you're single, the bigger your cojones."

My cojones shrank, but my heart grew the following year, when my sister Debbie and her husband invited me to attend a behavior modification seminar they were involved in. They promised if I went, I would be able to understand myself and to connect emotionally with my daughters. The seminar was a combination of self-discovery from different schools of thought.

The first day of the seminar opened my eyes, my heart, and my spirit to something I'd never acknowledged. I kept hearing the trainer ask, "What are you avoiding?," "Why are you avoiding it?," and, "What are you afraid of?" Over and over the trainer would tell us, "The only way out is through." Though I had no idea what any of this meant, I would soon find out.

During the training, I learned to receive honest and sometimes disturbing feedback about myself without becoming defensive. At the end of my first day, each of us went around the room telling every person in the training group how they "showed up" and what persona their appearance and body language were giving off. We were to listen to the feedback without responding. The information my peers offered about me left me surprised and shocked. More than one person said I seemed superficial, unapproachable, arrogant, and materialistic. Wow...anything else?! I couldn't believe what I heard and couldn't believe I had paid good money for this "mental training," which felt more like mental boot camp! It deeply hurt to hear people who didn't even know me make negative judgments about me. The character I was apparently revealing was not who I was on the inside. I was ready to change that. Throughout the three months of training, I began to learn I was using my outward perfectionism to protect myself from the pain of rejection, and in so doing, I learned not to feel or show emotions or trust myself.

I spent every weekend for the next three months learning the answers to these questions and many others and incorporating new ways of thinking and being into my life. I was ready to become emotionally available for my daughters and myself. I kept hearing the words, "Trust the process."

No longer able to hide behind my perfectionism, I ventured out of my comfort zone and let people from this seminar enter my most private and vulnerable places. Like an onion skin, one layer at a time I peeled back the layers of worldly lies I had believed and in time began my healing through my tears of truth.

To complete my journey of self discovery, a few of my team members and I signed up for a rain-or-shine trust-building field trip. And as luck would have it, it began drizzling and then pouring by the time we arrived. Putting my normally more chic persona aside, I cloaked myself in a yellow plastic poncho with matching pants, baseball cap, and athletic shoes. I hadn't any idea what I was going to be doing, but the instructor told us to "Be ready to stretch beyond your limits."

LIFE IS LIKE RIDING A BICYCLE. TO KEEP YOUR BALANCE YOU MUST KEEP MOVING.
—Albert Einstein[23]

Between the discomfort of my plastic ensemble and weather conditions, I felt more than stretched—similar to how I felt during my open water dive—only this time my feet were on solid ground, at least for the moment.

I got talked into a ropes course that took me way out of my comfort zone and beyond any physical achievement I had ever experienced on land. The goal of the exercise was to teach trust and teamwork. This exercise was challenging enough in good weather conditions, but in the rain it seemed almost impossible. Wanting to back out, I watched and waited while others on my team attempted this balancing act. Some conquered it and some did not. There was a battle going on in my head, but I was determined to win by balancing my fears and discomfort with the new trust and confidence I had gained. Plus, I didn't want to let my team down. The goal was to individually climb up twenty feet using the metal footholds on the tree, like a telephone repair person, and then cross

WHAT YOU FEAR
YOU CREATE;
WHATEVER YOU
FOCUS ON GROWS.
— DR. PHIL[24]

a rope bridge twenty feet off the ground. (This was not disclosed in the seminar brochure!) I was never the tomboy type, so climbing a tree at age forty-five in the wilderness in the rain and then crossing an open rope bridge with a partner took all the courage I could muster, even with safety cables. I started climbing up the tree. I was holding on with my wet hands trying to pull myself up to the platform and then wait for my partner, Joe, a buffed twenty-eight-year-old, to climb up and join me. Together we began crossing a rope bridge with wood plank steps spaced every two feet with nothing but air in between. While holding each other's hands for support, we slowly leaped across the open planks in unison, being careful not to lose our footing and fall to the ground. With each successful giant step, the rope bridge swayed back and forth, while our legs wobbled and our team cheered below. We were halfway across when we jumped together, and Joe lost his balance. One of his legs got stuck between the planks and was dangling through the bridge, threatening to pull us both to the ground. As our team gasped in fear and watched, I never let go of him, and it took all the strength and balance I could muster to keep him from pulling me down with him. As Joe slowly pulled himself back up, our team screamed with victory. We made it the rest of the way without anymore close calls or need for our safety cables, and although I looked like a drowned rat by the end of the day, I was elated when I had accomplished the course successfully.

While balancing my mind and controlling my thoughts during the ropes course, I had to use new tools from the training that allowed me to shift my thinking and to develop confidence. Learning how my conversations became my truth, I was taught to be careful of what I thought about and what I said to myself minute by minute.

APPLY YOUR MIND TO INSTRUCTION AND CORRECTION, AND YOUR EARS TO THE WORDS OF KNOWLEDGE.

—PROVERBS 23:12

Peeling away the layers and old conversations, I began to not only discover but also to truly believe that I am a powerful, loving, and courageous woman, and I deserve and am worthy of the best life has to offer.

By being honest and authentic during the training, I discovered it was safe to display my feelings and trust my instincts. I liked who I had become. I was no longer defined by my old survival strategies, which included looking good, being right, and being in control in order to avoid pain. These old strategies had ruled my life; I had been simply surviving life instead of thriving!

After I completed self-discovery training, I volunteered to coach the new recruits, which also helped reinforce my new ways of being. I heard the feedback and received thank-you notes from my graduates saying things like, "Thank you for being so vulnerable and approachable," "Your honesty and openness helped me learn more about myself," and, "You are beautiful on the outside, but even more so on the inside," This was the frosting on my cake!

LIFE INGREDIENT: BALANCE
BLONDIE BALANCE BARS

Believe it or not, there's no butter in these!

2 large eggs, at room
temperature
1¾ cups packed light brown
sugar
1 cup all-purpose flour
⅛ teaspoon baking soda
1 cup walnuts or pecans,
coarsely chopped

Caramel Frosting (to make
extra scrumptious!):
¼ cup brown butter
¼ cup dark-brown sugar
⅛ cup whole milk or half & half
1 cup confectioner's sugar

➤ Preheat oven to 350 degrees. Position one rack to center of oven.

➤ Line an 8 x 8 inch baking pan with parchment paper, leaving extra on the end as handles, making it easier to remove once baked.

➤ Whisk eggs in a medium bowl just until lightly beaten. Whisk in sugar until well blended, crushing any lumps against side of bowl. With wooden spoon, stir in flour, baking soda and walnuts (batter will be stiff and sticky).

➤ Spread evenly in prepared pan. Bake for 30 to 35 minutes until top golden and a wooden pick inserted in center comes out clean.

➤ Place pan on wire rack to cool 1 hour. Run a thin knife around inside edges of pan. Holding paper handles, lift blondies to cutting board and frost. Then cut and serve.

➤ Frosting: In a heavy-bottomed sauce pan melt butter on low heat, watching closely until lightly brown in color. Add brown sugar, stirring until the sugar is dissolved. Slowly add the milk and blend, do not boil. Stir in the powdered sugar. Pour over blondies and garnish with some chopped nuts. Frosting will dry as it cools.

Makes 16 large squares. Enjoy!

THANKS, OPRAH,
I NEEDED THAT!

Be thankful for what you have; you'll end up having more. If you concentrate on what you don't have, you will never, ever have enough.

—Oprah Winfrey

Changing your attitude to gratitude will help you overcome any of life's challenges. Gratitude is a key ingredient to satisfy your soul and create a life worth sharing! Focus on what you have in life. Stop comparing to others and worrying about tomorrow and start living for today. Light a candle instead of cursing the darkness and open your hands, your heart, and your soul to receive what's waiting—invisible but nonetheless real—just around the corner.

The big day had finally arrived. It was the first day of school, one of the happiest and most anticipated days of the year for most moms (and some kids.) Adele and Lindsay were up early that September morning, excited to be driving to high school together in Adele's new Infiniti, the nicest car in our driveway, thanks to the trust from their father's estate.

After the girls left for school, I finished loading my old Volvo wagon with the tasseled bedding, Tuscany art and mirrors, sculpted towels, carved candle holders, tapestry pillows, decorator pasta jars, designer soaps and potpourri, leather books, candlestick lamps, potted ivies, orchids, and orange tool box for a huge home staging job nearby. Barely able to see out my windows of my trusty wagon, I headed to the nearby Starbucks to get a Venti double-shot, non-fat, no-whip mocha to rev up my engine. As I walked up to place my order, I heard boisterous laughter coming from a nearby table. Many of the women sitting together were mothers of my daughters' friends from their high school. While waiting for my coffee, I overheard them planning lunch dates and shopping trips as they lingered leisurely over their coffee and pastries without a care in the world.

Leaving Starbucks that morning, I felt sorry for myself. My life seemed so arduous and unsatisfying at that moment, and it wasn't PMS talking. Being a single parent and breadwinner was exhausting and often extremely stressful. I found myself comparing my life to that of other women around me, thinking how much easier they had it. They were stay-at-home moms or had careers with supportive husbands, having what seemed to be a parachute of money from their families that would float them if they found themselves in a freefall.

As I enjoyed my pity party in my head, I drove to Alamo Springs, a spectacular neighborhood with Hollywood-type mansions where I was about to stage a fabulous home. Sitting in front of the Tuscany-style home, I forced myself to don my happy face and Home MakeOvers cap. With my buzz from my coffee high, I got to work.

GRATITUDE IS NOT ONLY THE GREATEST OF VIRTUES, BUT THE PARENT OF ALL OTHERS.

— MARCUS TULLIUS CICERO[25]

At the end of the day, after staging the forty-eight-hundred-square-foot multi-million dollar home for a couple of thirtysomething techie millionaires who were building a larger Tuscan villa nearby, I felt even more depressed and exhausted. As I packed up to leave, I overheard the couple worrying about whether their imported Italian hand-carved stone doors and windows would arrive on time. They debated whether they should have four or five fireplaces and then argued over which artisan they would hire to Venetian plaster their two-thousand-bottle wine room! These were major issues for them.

In contrast, my worries included making ends meet, providing enough TLC for my fatherless daughters, and never finding a partner with whom to share life's lessons, miracles, and sorrows. While wallowing in my discontent, I hosted another pity party for myself as I drove home, thinking my financial and relationship circumstances needed to change before I could become one hundred percent happy.

Once I had arrived at home, I unloaded the extra art, pillows, books, and pasta jars and put them back into the storage cabinets in my garage, breaking my favorite candlestick lamp in the process. Finally I collapsed on the sofa with my faithful furry companion, Bentley, our tenacious terrier, and I turned on the TV for a little escape before the girls came home from school. I stopped flipping channels when I heard Oprah Winfrey say, "An abundant life begins with gratitude."

"God will not bless you with more until you are satisfied and thankful for what you already have," her guest speaker added. "If you are living with worrying you can't be living with gratitude."

I felt as if they were both speaking directly to me, forcing me to think about my day, my attitude, and my life. I was filling my heart with worry, comparisons, and "shoulda coulda wouldas." I knew I wasn't feeling grateful for the many blessings I already had: my independence as an entrepreneur; my beautiful, strong daughters; a family that always supported me, my job, my strong body, my girlfriends, and of course my miracle home on Hope Lane. And I certainly wasn't trusting God to provide, even though He had been doing a pretty good job of it.

"God can only help those who help themselves," the guest speaker proclaimed.

I knew God could only make changes in me if I was willing to change my attitude. Once again, I had become the biggest hindrance to my own personal blessings. It was that afternoon that my "divine discontent" led to my transformation of gratitude.

Hearing what Oprah and her guest said had struck a nerve in my soul, and I began crying softly as Bentley comforted me with his dog kisses. Oprah suggested to her audience that they start gratitude journals, promising that by doing so their lives would transform. Ready to test her promise, I went out the next day and bought a special gratitude notebook, and at the end of each day I wrote down everything I was thankful for. At first my pages were half empty (or, depending on how you look at it, half full), but as months went by, I was filling the pages with blessings and answered prayers.

WE OFTEN TAKE FOR GRANTED THE VERY THINGS THAT MOST DESERVE OUR GRATITUDE.

— CYNTHIA OZICK[26]

Before long, I looked at each challenge in my life as an opportunity or learning experience, and I began to feel more thankful for my staging business, Home MakeOvers. Even though it was exhausting and unglamorous at times to replace my decorator hat with those of movers and cleaning people, I felt blessed to have the health, strength, and hardiness it took to climb ladders, hang pictures, and move furnishings from room to room. Plus, it was a great workout and easily burned off all the cookie calories I consumed.

In the upcoming weeks, I took my new attitude with me and with my mom as my design assistant. I drove into the Montclair

Hills to begin another large staging job. My mom was a great sport to help me out. I did most of the heavy lifting and moving, but I loved having her decorator eye to help me with the art and accessories. I had ordered a truck to deliver a very large painting from a nearby art gallery. It was priced at fifteen hundred dollars, but I was able to rent it for seventy-five dollars a month. This was a spectacular home, and it needed unique furnishings and art to enhance it, so I went for it. My staging expertise paid off, and the home sold within the first week, and for well over the asking price!

After the sale, Mom and I went back to the home to remove my decorator items so that the new owners could move in. I decided to forgo the added fee of seventy-five dollars to have the painting picked up, thinking I would add it to my profits by returning it myself. Using bungee cords, I began securing the painting to the top of my Volvo wagon since it was far too large to fit in the car. My mom spoke up to me in her strongest tone, saying, "Lori, don't be penny wise and pound foolish and risk all you've worked for. What if you damage this expensive art? Is it really worth the risk?"

Confidently I answered, "Don't worry, Mom, the gallery is only two freeway exits away, and with the extra profit we can celebrate with a gourmet lunch. I know what I'm doing." Ha!

As I approached fifty-five miles per hour and my exit, the painting started bouncing up and down against the top of my car, and within minutes, the five-foot canvas had flown off the top like a large square Frisbee. In my rearview mirror, I watched it land in the nearby weeds at the freeway off-ramp, and prayed for a miracle. I pulled over and walked back along the freeway to assess the damages. Hallelujah! The painting had landed face up, safe, and fully intact. I laughed nervously, shaking from fear as I realized the damage I could have done to another driver on top of ruining the beautiful painting and losing all of my profit.

At that moment, a truck stopped, and a contractor who had seen what happened jumped out to help me. He scolded me as he began securely tying the art to my car with enough rope to tie down a herd of cattle while teaching me the difference between bungee cords and ropes and the purpose of each. That painting wasn't going anywhere, except back to the gallery.

As we drove to the gallery, even though she was right, my mom never said, "I told you so," and I was so grateful for that kindness. I was even more thankful for the laws of aerodynamics and the contractor who rescued me, plus the lesson, "Penny wise and pound foolish!" Mom and I celebrated with gratitude over an indulgent gourmet lunch, and we laughed about the flying painting all the way home. After the flying painting episode and another exhausting week of staging, I found another reason to feel grateful when friends invited me to go skiing over the upcoming weekend. Looking forward to a much-needed break, I gladly accepted their invitation.

The first day had been perfect, and I surprised my friends (and myself) with my skiing skills after having been more than ten years off the slopes. At the end of that perfect day, I took one last run, practically flying down the hill, laughing, and skiing confidently towards the lodge. Suddenly I fell over a mogul and heard the pop. My knee went one way, and my ski went the other! No one thought I had hurt anything because my sunglasses were still in place. I stood up and I tried to ski down but couldn't because of the severe pain and instability of my knee. My friends had to ski down to get help for me. I ended up going down the hill on my back, humiliated and strapped into the ski patrol's toboggan basket, unable to enjoy the ride or even the handsome skier who helped me.

The X-rays at the ski resort showed no broken bones, which I was grateful for. But by the time I got home, my boney knee had become the size of a Texas grapefruit. The MRI revealed a severed ACL tendon and the meniscus torn in a couple places. I was shocked when the doctor told me I had two surgical choices in order to repair and stabilize my knee. The first choice involved reconstructing an ACL from my healthy hamstring tendon, requiring a five-inch surgical incision and further pain and recovery time. My second choice was to use a cadaver's ACL and attach it with two headless screws with minimal incisions and hope my body would not reject it.

I WILL THANK YOU LORD WITH ALL MY HEART; I WILL TELL OF ALL THE MARVELOUS THINGS YOU HAVE DONE.

—PSALM 9:1

I hobbled out of the doctor's office on my crutches, feeling worse and more anxious than when I had hobbled in. Grateful for my resource of wonderful girlfriends, I called one of my best friends, Pattie, a highly skilled ER nurse whom I had known since kindergarten. Pattie had seen it all, and so I respected her opinion and knew she would give me sound advice. After hanging up the phone with Pattie and doing more research, I opted for door number two, praying I would get the biggest, baddest, and strongest cadaver ACL tendon possible and that my body would love it.

The three-and-a-half-hour surgery proved successful! Sweet sister Debbie, who is also an RN, accompanied me home. Everything was fine until the pain pills wore off, and I began throwing up from the anesthesia. More pain pills, please!

Between the excruciating pain from surgery, the two screws in my knee, the large brace and noisy ice machine attached to my left knee at night, it was impossible to rest. I spent most of my day stuck on the sofa in a brace, my knee attached to either the ice machine or the painful PRM exercise machine. My cocktail table was covered with medical equipment, pain pills, magazines, and books, and I could see how alarmed my friends and family were when they came to visit. No one had ever seen me this vulnerable and helpless. All I wanted to do was get back to work, start climbing ladders, schlepping accessories, and moving furniture. I told myself that I would be eternally grateful for all of those things if I could just get back to work!

I had to go to Physical Therapy (PT) three times a week, where I got to know many of the other patients who were recovering, many much worse off than I. We all commiserated about our injuries and our slow and steady recovery. And after about six weeks of PT, I could bend my knee enough to achieve a full but painful rotation on the stationary bicycle, bringing me to joyful tears. Six more months went by, but I was still complaining of pain. My doctor discovered another meniscus tear in my knee. Back under the knife I went, only this time for about an hour.

After living through two knee surgeries and months of crutches and physical therapy, I have a new appreciation for my body. I can finally climb ladders and enjoy spin classes with minimal pain and occasional knee popping. I am one of the lucky ones. Gratitude!

Now my heart goes out to those who live in chronic pain, knowing how hard it is to be grateful for anything when all you want is relief. Thankful for this painful lesson, I have learned to be kinder to myself and more tolerant towards others with physical ailments.

Looking back, I am thankful for all I have gone through: the good, the bad, and the painful. It has been during the hardest of times that I have learned and relearned the crucial life lessons that have made me the woman I am today.

Through the hard and sad times, and with God's help, my heart and spirit has been able to change for my benefit as well as for others'. My dream and God's plan for this next chapter of my life could only happen when my attitude had changed to gratitude.

Grateful

LIFE INGREDIENT: GRATITUDE
Grateful Granola Bars

7 cups old fashioned oats
½ cup vegetable oil
½ teaspoon salt
1 cup honey
¾ cup brown sugar, firmly
   packed
1 Tablespoon vanilla
3 teaspoons cinnamon
¼ cup flaxseed meal

1½ cups whole almonds, pecans,
   peanuts, or walnuts, coarsely
   chopped
1/3 cup coconut, shredded
½ cup diced dried fruit
1/3 cup sunflower seeds,
   unsalted
¾ cup white or chocolate chips*
   (optional)

Note: Quick-cooking oats cannot be substituted for the old-fashioned oats here because their texture becomes too sandy when toasted.

➤ Preheat oven to 350 degrees.

➤ Toss the oats, oil, and salt together in a medium bowl. Spread the mixture out over a baking sheet and toast in the oven, stirring often, until pale golden, 20 minutes. Let cool.

➤ Reduce the oven temperature to 300 degrees.

➤ Meanwhile, line an 18- x 13-inch rimmed baking sheet with parchment paper allowing it to hang over the ends.

➤ In a small saucepan, cook honey and sugar together over medium heat, stirring frequently, until the sugar is fully dissolved, about 5 minutes. Remove from heat, add the vanilla and cinnamon, stir to mix. Cool slightly.

➤ Transfer the cooled, toasted oat mixture to a large bowl and toss with honey mixture, and remaining ingredients, except chips*. After slight cooling, add chips. *Note: If adding white or chocolate chips, cool honey mixture first or it will melt the chocolate when added in the next step.*

➤ Spread the mixture out over the prepared pan and press firmly into an even layer using a greased spatula.

➤ Bake the granola bars until golden, 35 to 40 minutes. Rotate pan halfway through baking.

➤ Remove from oven and let bars cool in the pan for 15 minutes, then cut into bars.

➤ Let the bars cool completely, then remove individual bars from pan and serve.

Makes 36 large bars. Enjoy! To make ahead: the bars can be individually wrapped tightly in plastic wrap and stored at room temperature for up to 2 weeks.

LET THE GAMES BEGIN . . .

There are three things that will endure – faith,
hope, and love – and the greatest of these is Love.
—*I Corinthians 13:13*

I believe that every person can find love, but in order to do so you must first figure out what you need. What are the essential, nonnegotiable ingredients? Once you determine that, you must seek out those ingredients, making sure not to leave any out. Only then will you be able to create your recipe for happiness, blending someone else's qualities with your own.

I wish I could share my recipe with you—but you must create your own.

In my case, it took a bowl of discipline, a portion of passion, a pinch of faith, an ounce of forgiveness, a cup of courage, a *ladle of hope, a tablespoon of humor, a teaspoon of balance, and a sifter of gratitude in order to finally create my recipe for a life worth sharing—one that would satisfy the sweet tooth of my soul!*

The English language has only *one* word for the feeling of love, and that is . . . *LOVE.*

We get from the Greeks several words and meanings for love, including agape love.

The word *agape* often refers to unconditional love, regardless of circumstances. Some recognize this as the greatest of all loves, the love God has for each one of us. The unconditional love we get from our pets is a small measure of agape love, and Bentley was no exception.

He arrived in 1994 on Christmas Eve. The cutest West Highland white terrier ever. And boy, did he know he was cute! Adele and Lindsay were seven and nine, and I had been divorced from their dad for about four years. Bentley came all the way from Oregon and was a bundle of fluff, full of love and tenacity. He was Adele and Lindsay's favorite Christmas gift, and mine too. Bentley became my angel and my protector, especially during my single parenting years, when we took him everywhere. When he saw his leash, he became a wiggly-tail-wagging, bouncing ball. He loved being with us and was a great traveler; we took him on road trips, to concerts in the park, to the beach, in the snow, and camping. Bentley was always up for a family gathering or outdoor parties and would happily dress the part: flower lei for a backyard luau, stars and stripes for Fourth of July, and jingle bells for Christmas.

He always appreciated the new squeaker toys I brought home for him and drove us crazy with the noise. But such a happy noise it was! That sweet dog gave more love to us than we ever gave to him. From morning to night, on good days or bad, Bentley's eyes and tail showed how delighted he was to see me. If I was angry, sad, or crying at my bedside, he would find me and snuggle up close, licking my hands gently to comfort me.

Bentley's sweet and joyful spirit, smile, and big sparkling eyes were always there for us, and I only wish he hadn't left us so soon. When he started losing weight, he also started losing the spring in his step; the vet said the cancer was throughout his body and untreatable. No longer did he run for the new toys. Instead I would bring them to him to chew on as he lay in his bed. He also stopped caring about the doggie treats I would bring home, and he eventually stopped caring about his favorite meal. All he wanted was to lie by my side once I finally slowed down at the end of my day.

It was so hard watching him get thinner and weaker. One night after sitting together on the sofa, I put him into his bed, and he died that night in his sleep. He was just eleven years old. I will always wonder if Bentley may have absorbed some of the pain and struggles I was going through. My happiness and comfort were his main concern, which is why I have compared the unconditional love of our pets to the agape love of God.

I believe God put domestic pets on this earth to both teach us and bless us! We can learn so much about love and acceptance from our furry children. Maybe that's why "dog" spelled backwards is "god." The older I become, the more I cherish animals and what they teach us.

After Bentley died, although I missed him terribly, I finally felt as if I had my life together. At forty-six, I had learned to love myself and all I had been through—home, job, and surroundings. I had an abundant life and felt truly blessed and grateful for all I had and all I had accomplished. The only thing missing was someone to share it with, and I was ready to find that love for the last time.

I didn't date for almost a year after my divorce from Chip but instead put all my energy into Adele and Lindsay, getting back into real estate, and building my staging business. I was afraid of making another wrong choice in men. I had decorating, baking, and business instincts, but not the dating instincts I needed. I just never realized how unprepared I was for the dating scene and wasn't too eager to find out.

My married friends said it was easy to meet great men, but all the exceptional men they knew just happened to be taken. My single friends often said they were looking for love, but they seemed pretty content staying single and partying all night. I was usually the last to show up and the first to leave their singles' party or bar scene. It was always the same old scene and people, and I usually couldn't wait to get out of my "single clothes" and into my "comfy clothes" back home. The singles scene was how I had met my first and second mates, and I realized that was no way to meet the husband I was now looking for. That scene always turned out to be a waste of time and calories, and most of the time I ended up talking more to the bartender than anyone else.

When my neighbor Randy suggested I come over for dinner to meet his best friend, Bob, I agreed. *At least it was better than the single scene, and I can always walk home, if I'm bored.*

Bob was tall, tan, and balding, with a great big smile and boisterous Texas accent. He was playful, loved to joke around, and acted like a big kid. He was anything but boring and made me laugh constantly. A self-confessed food and wine enthusiast, he drove a Range Rover with a special refrigerator in the back filled with expensive champagne and imported chocolates—a man after my own heart. We really hit it off.

Bob told me he had a great position in the tech industry, but when the NASDAQ tanked, so had his job. He said he was in touch with a headhunter but hadn't found just the right thing yet. I knew a red flag when I saw one, but everything else about him seemed so right, so I ignored it and decided to give him a chance. I seemed to have forgotten my personal credo about red flags!

With an abundance of time on his hands, Bob generously helped me with the physical labor of my staging jobs. He loved cooking dinner for my daughters and me when I came home exhausted. My daughters really liked him, and so did my family and friends. They all thought we were a good match except for one thing: he needed a real j-o-b. While we dated, Bob never seemed to have money concerns, and for the next eight months, while he worked on getting a job we still enjoyed season tickets to games, hosting dinner parties with our friends, sharing rare wines from his wine collection, and going to the latest concerts. I ignored the job flag.

Things were going along smoothly until the night of my forty-seventh birthday. We had been dating for about ten months, and he was picking me up to take me to dinner at The French Laundry, one of the best restaurants in the Napa Valley. It had taken months to get reservations.

When I opened the front door, Bob handed me a bouquet of yellow roses and a small Tiffany box as he carried in a chilled bottle of my favorite French champagne. He gave me a big Texas kiss, telling me, "I hope you know I would do anything for you. You are my world!" I laughed and began to close the front door. I stopped as I noticed an old beige, beat-up BMW parked near the front of my house.

Whose car is that? Maybe I should call the police. Oh well, if it's still here when we're back from Napa, I'm calling a tow truck. I was annoyed.

Bob closed the door quickly. "It's time for bubbles, birthday girl. Let's pop this cork!"

As we sipped champagne, he toasted me and looked into my eyes and said, "I look forward to spending many more birthdays together with you, Lori Jayne. You are the love of my life."

Then he asked me to open the gift he had brought me, but I told him I'd like to wait and open it at the restaurant. After we shared another glass of champagne, it was time to go.

I was famished and couldn't believe we were going to be dining at the famous French Laundry Restaurant. As we walked outside, I noticed my empty driveway. No car of Bob's. "Where's your Range Rover, Bob?" I asked.

Bob grabbed my shoulders and stared at me with tears in his eyes. "There's something I should have told you by now, sweetheart. I've kind of been living off my father's trust fund this past year, and now, quite unexpectedly, I'm told it has run out of money. My Range Rover got repossessed when I couldn't make the payments, so I've had to resort to my old college Beamer. But I'll find a great job soon and lease another one. Things will work out. I promise, Baby."

I stood frozen as he walked over to his old beat-up BMW—the same one I planned to have towed—and opened the door for me to get in. Standing there, I saw patches on the old leather seats, worn maps, papers falling out of the door pockets, and what looked like unopened mail and bills hanging from the visors.

WE COME TO LOVE NOT BY FINDING A PERFECT PERSON, BUT BY LEARNING TO SEE AN IMPERFECT PERSON PERFECTLY.
—SAM KEEN[27]

"I can't do this." I whispered, to myself at first. "I've been down this road before. I can't wait for you to be ready!" My voice grew louder as I continued. "I can't make you into someone you're not!" By now I was screaming. "I can't ignore the *BIG, FAT RED FLAG WAVING IN FRONT OF MY FACE!*"

Bob just stood there with his mouth hanging open, having no idea of what I was ranting about.

I threw my birthday gift into his shabby, scruffy car and stormed into my house, slamming the front door. I grabbed the remaining champagne and plopped down on my bed as I realized that I had spent the past ten months with an impostor.

Another year had gone by, another unsuccessful attempt at love, and I was no closer to meeting my match. Would I ever learn? How many flags does it take?

The disciplined goal setter that I am made me determined to learn how to date, find love, build a partnership, and be married by the time I became a half-century old. I figured that if I could change cookie history a quarter of a century earlier, creating the first white chocolate macadamia cookie and building a cookie empire of seventy stores in five years, I could certainly find my husband and lifetime partner in three.

I started my search in earnest. I began reading relationship and dating books, which didn't prepare me for the realities of dating in my late forties during the twenty-first century. All the rules had changed since high school and college. I couldn't find any books geared towards women my age.

Then I saw an ad for a dating service where you meet for lunch. They claimed to help busy professional singles meet other busy professionals through a lunch date. Lunch sounded like a fun way to meet, so I called the number and said, "Sign me up!"

"How wonderful to have you with us, Lori," said the perky woman on the other end of the line. But when I called after that to ask if they had any prospects for me, they rarely knew who I was. Their staff changed frequently, and I would have to reintroduce myself again and again. Months went by, and after just a few awkward, incompatible lunch dates, I bagged the service and went back to brown-bagging my lunch. I needed a personal touch.

As time went on, I yearned for the physical touch of a warm and loving man. I decided to hire a local matchmaker who was advertised in all the best local magazines. After she pocketed the fifteen-hundred-dollar fee, Margaret the matchmaker, with her coiffed hair, overly large breasts, fake eyelashes, and long, red nails promised to find me "Mr. Right." We met for an extensive two-hour interview where she took profuse notes, asking me about the characteristics I was looking for in my perfect mate, asking me to close my eyes and envision this person as she jotted down my answers about his age, height, weight, hair color, education, profession, income, political affiliation, religion, ages of kids if any, and sexual frequency. When we finished the interview, Margaret asked me to fill out a questionnaire with many of the same questions I had just answered.

Three hours later, I walked out of her office exhausted as she waved to me, saying, "Get your beauty sleep, honey, and get ready for your knight in shining armor!"

Finally, I was on the right track. When Margaret called about my first match, I was so excited. She described him as perfect for me. "He's tall, handsome, successful, and a stimulating conversationalist," she said. "He lives in San Francisco and would love to meet you for dinner.

His name is James."

"Tell me when and where." I was excited.

As I walked into the intimate Italian restaurant in Orinda, I saw an average-looking man with thinning hair and a nice smile looking my way. He waved at me, stood up, and introduced himself as James. "At least he's tall," I thought. We ordered an appetizer and started sharing about ourselves and our lives. As I nibbled on the calamari, the subject of politics and religion came up, and when I heard his comments, I knew we weren't a match . .. at all.

Throughout dinner I felt like I was on a debate team; sparring with each other about every controversial subject under the sun, from Darwinism versus creationism to liberal versus conservative, even cats versus dogs. Feeling indigestion from all the stimulation, I thanked James for a very invigorating evening, then walked to my car, popped a Tums, and headed home.

I couldn't wait to call Margaret the following day but didn't have to because early the next morning, she called me. "I heard you two really hit it off last night."

We almost hit each other.

"James wants to know if I he can have your phone number. He wants another date with you, Lori. He finds you stimulating and loves your energy!" she said excitedly.

"Heaven knows I love a good debate, Margaret, but I certainly don't want a lifetime of it," I said.

I had learned from a wise counselor during my marriage with Chip who had said, "Opposites do attract, but they make for a very hard marriage." Twice I had married my opposite, and I decided I would never do that again.

"Please take a good look at your notes, and don't call me with another date unless you find someone who matches me ninety-nine out of one hundred." I hung up the phone. *What a waste of my evening, my new outfit, and fifteen hundred dollars.*

Almost a month had gone by before I heard from Margaret again. This time when she called, she promised I wouldn't be disappointed. "Peter has it all," she said confidently, "looks, money, similar values, grown kids, a nice ex, and a dog."

"Great," I said, pleased. He sounded a little too good to be true. "When and where do I meet him?" I asked.

Margaret arranged our lunch date for the following Saturday.

Putting on my designer jeans and cream silk shirt, I drove to a casual café in Pleasanton. After I waited at the bar for eighteen minutes while getting more and more annoyed, a gorgeous guy wearing designer workout clothes jogged over to me. "You must be Lori. I'm Peter," he said, squeezing my hand. "Sorry I'm a little late, but better late than never."

That was a rude thing to say. I knew trouble was on the horizon.

The minute we sat, he signaled the waitress and declared, "I'm starving."

The waitress handed us two menus. Before I could read through the daily specials, Peter had closed his menu. "I'm ready to order, are you?"

"I guess I am," I said, closing the menu.

As I sat across from him I noticed Peter's thick salt-and-pepper hair, ice-blue eyes and tan chiseled face. *He is definitely handsome,* I decided. *At least Margaret got that right.*

And for the next hour, Peter began sharing all about himself and his life as I listened, waiting for him to ask about mine. He talked about his job in commercial real estate, his home in Pleasanton, his passion of sailing, and his spiritual beliefs and political views, both which were similar to mine. Then I heard about his two amazing grown sons, his fabulous ex-wife, and his golden retriever, Max. Just as I was about to interject about myself, my job, and my two wonderful daughters, his cell phone rang, and he answered it!

"Yes. No. We won't negotiate. ninety-eight million, firm." He hung up. "Sorry, it was business. Now where was I?"

"Actually, Peter, I can't believe how fast the time went." I fibbed. "I have another appointment I have to get to," I said, signaling the waitress.

While we waited for the bill, Peter continued sharing more stories about his favorite subject— Peter! And as we stood outside the restaurant, Peter grabbed my hand and said, "It's weird, I feel like I've known you for years. I feel a connection and chemistry and would love to see you again, Lori."

Connection? He didn't even know what I do for a living or where I live or that I have two great daughters or that I love dogs. He did not know one single thing about me, because he never cared enough to ask.

"Just call Margaret," I said to Peter as I walked across the street to my car. Next!

When Margaret called the following morning, she sounded almost giddy. "Peter called and said you two connected in a special way, and he wants your phone number, Lori. Shall I give it to him?"

"No," I said emphatically. "Don't give him or anyone else my name, my number, my e-mail or my picture. Your service doesn't work for me, Margaret. I would love my money back."

"That wasn't part of the agreement," she quickly interjected. "You're not an easy one to match, Lori," She was irritated.

Ignoring her tone, I continued. "Please take me off your files, your rolodex and your computer Web site. I'm taking over now, but thanks for helping me finally figure things out."

As I hung up the phone, I actually felt relieved. I had to become more proactive. As the saying goes, "God helps those who help themselves."

I realized I needed to be the top chef in my own kitchen, screening and then choosing whom I wanted to meet. No one knew me or what I was looking for, better than I so I had to figure this out on my own.

Digging through my dresser drawer, I pulled out a description of my perfect match that I had written and tucked away on May 28, 2002, after an evening of champagne therapy and a year after divorcing Chip. I never would have written it if not for one of my best girlfriends, Tammy, who shared her secret for finding her mate by telling me, "You must visualize and write down everything you're looking for in your perfect match, before you'll ever find him—including what he looks like, what he does for a living, his personality and hobbies. You have to visualize what you want before you'll ever find it."

So here is what I really wrote:

He will be tall, probably more brunette than blonde.
He will smile a lot, laugh a lot.
He'll have a zest for life.
He will work hard, probably in contracting or finance.
He will have influence and be highly respected.
He will have financial success.
He will love to travel…first class whenever possible, yet will be humble and down to earth.
He will be spiritual and sensual.
He will be thankful and show gratitude to his family and all he works with.
He will have some great male friends with fun wives.
He will probably golf, like hanging out with some guy friends, but of course love being with me the most.
He will love to dance and work out and be physically fit but not fanatical.
He will love to cook special meals, barbecuing, or just helping me in the kitchen.
He will love our home and fixing it up.
He will have a great appreciation for fine homes, fine amenities, and fine architecture.
He will love me and my daughters generously with a love that brings out the best in us and makes us feel protected and cherished.
Our love will be powerful. We will compliment each other's character.
We will be soul mates.
We will be great separately, but even greater together.
We will be in love.
He will know, and I will know it is forever.
I hope I will meet him soon!

It was August 2004, and I was ready to test my formula.

I decided to join Match.com because I had met a few people at work who had actually met their significant other from Match. They said it was user friendly, and I would see specific details such as height, income, children, religion, and hobbies before I agreed to e-mail, talk by phone, or meet in person.

Let the games begin!

Almost immediately, I began to receive lots of winks and flattering male attention daily via e-mail. It was overwhelming and a little scary to think my profile and photos were out in cyberspace for all to see, but I diligently read through each of the e-mails and sent back my usual "Thanks for your interest in me, you look like a great guy, but from our profiles I can see we're not a match."

WHERE THERE IS GREAT LOVE, THERE ARE ALWAYS MIRACLES.

—WILLA SIBERT CATHER[28]

After months of winks, e-mails and a few mismatched dates over coffee or a glass of wine where there was no hope for a second, I realized my profile was not specific enough. I kept getting responses from men who really didn't know what they were looking for.

I knew I was looking for a mind, body, and soul connection, but I needed to spell out what that meant to me. I finally knew who I was and what the necessary ingredients were in my recipe for life, but now I had to identify the key ingredients I needed in my recipe for love.

So, this is what I cooked up for my profile:

MINDBODYSOULMATE is looking for happily ever after . . .

I am a passionate, positive, sensual, and spontaneous woman. I lead a balanced, healthy lifestyle filled with my family, my friends and my work. I believe in honesty, loyalty, kindness, and hard work and have a true appreciation for the finer things in life. My lifestyle is casual elegance . . . I love black-tie, but am much more comfortable in my jeans!

I love to laugh . . . and can even laugh at myself! I love wine-tasting, entertaining, dancing, traveling, and just being with my best friend and forever lover. I am a hopeful romantic and believe in happily-ever-after. I love to be spoiled and adored, and I love to spoil those I love. I am very generous emotionally and physically . . . there must be chemistry. I am an imperfect Christian woman who is committed to spiritual and personal growth and I want a partner who shares similar beliefs and wants to grow as well. I don't expect or ask for anything I too am not willing to give or do. My partner must have healthy, not codependent, relationships with his family and friends and know the difference! He must be financially responsible and have a healthy balance between work and play. A giver, not a taker, with a positive, can-do attitude and a great sense of humor!

No victims allowed! He must be able to share his feelings with me and be emotionally available. A man who is not afraid to be vulnerable: true intimacy, not just in the bedroom, an intimate and whole partnership of one-hundred-one-hundred. My children are grown, and their father is deceased. I am at a time in my life where I finally know who I am and what I want. I am looking for a man who wants to be "in love" and married for the last time . . . "till death do us part." Please be honest with yourself and me and do not contact me unless you truly believe we could be a match!

PS: A "mean" BBQ is a plus!

I got an email from *ADVENTUROUSANDROMANTIC* on Valentine's Day 2005.

Dave wrote that he would like to meet me as soon as possible. When I checked out his profile, he had answered all the questions thoroughly, and I really liked what I read. From his photos I could see he was tan and brunette with a nice smile and met my height requirement. So far, so good.

His profile said:

> *If what you desire is to be in a romantic relationship with a gentleman of character who is intelligent, physically active, sensitive, and sexy, then I just might be what you're looking for. I have a proactive attitude, always looking at the glass as half full, seeing the good in others and in situations. I like to make special times out of the ordinary, to plan nice picnics or candlelight dinners for two. I love to cook and enjoy being romantic, and I'm not afraid to show my affections. Being physically active, I take care of myself and exercise regularly, enjoying spin classes, and yoga, with snow skiing in the winter and waterskiing in the summer. I am a man with many life experiences, light on the baggage, well balanced and secure, taking pride in everything I do. I am a man of my word with honesty and integrity. I am looking to meet a quality woman with a little more style than most. A woman who is physically active and emotionally secure who would be interested in sharing, discovering, and exploring all life has to offer—someone who is not afraid to get out and try new things. I find the best part of living in Sacramento is that it is so close to so many wonderful places to get away for the day or the weekend. Would you like to go and check out a few of them together?*

He sounded like the male version of me, only more adventurous.

He e-mailed me and said he was a hard-working Christian man who loved his grown son and family very much. He said he loved to cook and entertain, was very good with tools, and had even built his own home. In fact, he was hosting an Easter brunch for twenty members of his family.

The only problem I could see from his profile was that he was geographically undesirable, residing far beyond my fifteen-mile radius criteria. In fact, he was one-and-a-half hours north of me. So, before I even agreed to have a first date with him, we talked on the phone, and I shared my concerns about getting involved. I told him I was finally settled and not willing to move away from my daughters anytime soon. He told me he loved the area where I lived and would be willing to relocate if it worked out between us. Another perfect answer!

We had our first date on February 20, 2005.

We met for lunch at one of my favorite restaurants on a rainy Sunday. He arrived early and had a beautiful bouquet of French tulips in a vase waiting for me he had picked up from my favorite florist in the area (unbeknownst to him). We talked over lunch as he shared his life story with me and opened up about his faith in God, revealing how it had saved him. He became teary as he shared his first very hard lesson in forgiveness for his father who had committed suicide when Dave was only fourteen. He told me how much he had loved his dad, and the pain from this horrendous event showed on his face. Overnight he was forced to go from a child to a man, and his courage to overcome this tragedy amazed me. He went to work at that young age with his mother and sisters looking to him as the man of the house. Later he quit college and moved away to work in commercial construction, becoming a foreman at twenty. Dave didn't seem afraid or intimated by anything or anyone.

We discovered we were in sync concerning the big things like morality, spirituality, and politics. And we shared family values. Over dessert and coffee we realized we had similar tastes in furnishings, foods, and lifestyles. In fact, he loved Middle Eastern foods since his mother is half Lebanese. I wasn't overly attracted to him at first—his complexion was rough, showing years of a very hard life— but I loved his beautiful blue eyes that sparkled with kindness when he smiled and laughed. Many things about our relationship seemed right, as if God had brought us together.

But I didn't think he was acting very godly when after walking me to my car, he kissed me passionately! I told him that was totally inappropriate for a first date, but then I drove home thinking about him, our similarities, and the inappropriateness of a French kiss on a first date. We agreed to meet again the following weekend for a second date, and he called me many times during the week just to say hi. I had my radar up and was watching for any negative signs or red flags. Dave kept his word about when he would call. I had discovered that if there was dishonesty about anything, there should never, ever be a second date. It's like baking with artificial ingredients or rancid nuts; you'll end up tainting your real and fresh ingredients, compromising your recipe and wasting your time.

Our second date was for dinner in San Francisco, and Dave asked me to dress up. Since I'm not a big fan of dresses, I went casual elegant: black pants, silk blouse, pink pashmina, and my favorite jewelry. He arrived promptly at seven with a beautiful mixed bouquet and in suit and tie. I took him on a tour of my home, and he was very impressed with my eclectic style of decorating and the French antiques I adored. He told me how similar our styles and furnishings were and that he had French antiques at his home as well. I smiled skeptically, thinking he couldn't possibly know how to decorate too, could he?

Off to the city we went in his low, loud black Porsche—one of my least favorite cars—a pink flag in my dating world. I've never been a fan of hugging or feeling the road. Cars that are cushy and easy to get in and out of are more my style, but his profile had said, "adventurous."

He proceeded to take me on a "progressive dinner" in San Francisco. We began at Bacar for appetizers, then had our main course at Plouf, and enjoyed dessert and coffee at Cosmos. Dave was out to impress, and he was doing a good job of it. Except for the Porsche, we were compatible in most ways. After valet parking three times in one evening, I was glad I had worn slacks!

As we drove home, Dave told me he had booked a room at the Best Western in town so he wouldn't have to drive home late that night. He asked whether he could bring over coffee and pastries from Starbucks in the morning. With a gentle kiss goodnight, off he went to the Best Western. After a few more wonderful dates with Dave, I took my profile off Match.com. The more time I spent with him, the more I saw he was a close match to what I was looking for. Overall, he seemed to fit within all my key ingredients.

Dave appeared to live his life with discipline and balance. He loved his work in commercial construction as senior project manager and was disciplined enough to save for a fabulous vacation or gourmet experience. He was low maintenance when it came to his physical needs (like having his hair cut at Super Cuts). He had a sense of humor and could laugh at himself as he sang out boldly at church or danced with abandon to rock songs. Balance in life was very important to him, and at the end of each work week he would make time to celebrate life with friends, food, and fun. He loved planning weekend getaways for us and even packed picnic lunches, complete with fine wine and china. Dave had learned how to plant the roses, smell the roses, and then cut and arrange them beautifully in a crystal vase. I loved how he took time to show gratitude along the way. As difficult as his life had been growing up, he gave thanks to God each day.

Over the next three months, we began a whirlwind courtship. Because we loved so many of the same activities, we stayed busy every minute from dinner parties with friends and family to wine-tasting in Napa. And because of the two-hour commute from my house to his, we didn't spend much time on a day-to-day basis getting to know each other and just *being* together. Dave and I had so much fun *doing* that we never talked much about our feelings, our pasts, or past relationships. When past experiences arose, they weren't discussed with any depth, and we glossed over them just enough to scratch the surface before moving on to planning our next adventure together. I always yearned to dig deeper with Dave, but he just wasn't interested. Red flag, maybe?

In my heart, I believed we both wanted the same thing from our relationship: a mind, body, and soul connection. After all, I had spelled out exactly who I was and what I was looking for on my profile! I was getting so tired of going through the daily paces of life alone—sleeping alone, cooking alone, and church alone, plus my financial nut was getting harder and harder to crack each month. Deep inside, there was still a part of me that wanted someone to take care of me.

So on the day Dave told me he had been searching for me for seven years of his life, I believed what I was hearing and the love I was feeling. I needed and wanted Dave in my life and I desperately hoped there was a happily ever after ending for me. I excitedly answered "yes" that day Dave asked me to marry him. I was forty-nine years old. It had taken me three years of intentional dating (augmented by God's assistance) to find my match.

Dave immediately put his house on the market. He was so excited about moving my direction and finding new employment. From that moment on, we began planning our intimate wine-country wedding and the honeymoon we both had dreamed of.

I knew there were important details of our relationship we still needed to work out, like a prenuptial agreement, assets, and the premarital counseling I wanted us to schedule. I even signed us up for a communication seminar at my church, which we never attended. We had a Napa wedding and Greek honeymoon to plan and Dave's house to sell, so we put those other matters on the back burner. I picked up my favorite rose-colored glasses and proceeded with our to-do list, ignoring a possible red flag. There were menus to taste, flowers to choose, flights to schedule and a drop-dead dress to find. We would get to the other issues. *So I thought.*

Our September wedding day was a dream come true for me. The weather was glorious, the flowers romantic, and our vows brought tears and laughter to our family and friends in attendance. Everything was perfect, and I was even having a great hair day! I had finally found my happily-ever-after.

Then off to Greece we went to begin our adventurous honeymoon, where we were almost arrested—but that's another story for another book! Spending the next sixteen days together twenty-four-seven gave me the chance to try to talk with Dave about deeper issues in life, memories from our pasts, and hopes and dreams of our future. But past feelings weren't comfortable for Dave, and he preferred smelling the roses in Greece, enjoying restaurants, and sightseeing. He would become annoyed with me as I probed for deeper responses. I started feeling frustrated and disconnected with his superficial small talk. After all, I wanted a mind, body, and soul connection. Dave and I began to argue about some of the simplest things, from the best baklava to asking for directions while driving lost on our rented scooter. Dave began discovering that not only did I have strong opinions and feelings on subjects, but I really loved shopping. I especially loved the "smell of a jewelry store!" So, at a charming shop in Santorini, after Dave and I kissed and made up, he bought me a beautiful Greek eternity ring to remind me that I had promised I had changed my name for the last time. I reminded Dave of words of wisdom from one of my favorite movies, *My Big Fat Greek Wedding*: "The man may be the head of the household, but the woman is the neck, and we all know the neck turns the head!" He just laughed, but I now realize he probably did not agree.

We said goodbye to Greece, and as soon as we arrived back home, we hit the ground running. Dave's house sold the week we returned, and we began packing and moving his beautiful furnishings, multiple sets of dishes and serving pieces, countless tools, and an abundance of clothes into my modest home on Hope Lane. After adding shelves, hooks, and storage cabinets, we still could not fit Dave's entire household into my home, so we rented a storage unit for the overflow. With everything finally in its place, we settled in as empty-nesters and then decided to grow our family and expand my home. We brought home Harry and Sally, two West Highland white terrier puppies, almost as cute as Bentley. A month later we began remodeling and enlarging my home to make it ours.

We decided Dave needed his own office, and I needed my own closet, and our master bedroom and bath just didn't seem large enough for the both of us. So after hiring an engineer, drawing up plans, and planning our budget, we refinanced the mortgage and Dave's name went on the title. Dave was so disciplined and organized, and since I really didn't like paperwork, I agreed for him take charge of our finances and budget, putting my trust in him.

We had been married about four months when we began the eight-hundred-square-foot addition to our home, opening the back and side of our home during what turned out to be one of the rainiest winter seasons. This was not in our plan. Sleeping in the guest bedroom with dust everywhere and plastic sheeting protecting us from the weather outside was stressful and uncomfortable. With our strong opinions from prior remodeling experiences, it sometimes became a battle of our wills as differing views and budgets flew back and forth, like a contractor flinging his hammer. We were both writing checks from our separate accounts as we went over budget, trying to create our vision of hope. Finally the dust settled from our remodel, and another year flew by as we celebrated every holiday in our hope-filled home. Our end result was beautiful even if it did leave some battle scars on our marriage and our checkbook. I felt we had become two human doings, and we felt more like roommates or business partners than soul mates. All we seemed to talk or argue about was money or projects.

I wasn't feeling an emotional connection to Dave. As I looked at my dwindled savings account, I was starting to feel vulnerable and very naïve. I knew with our combined incomes we always paid the bills, but I realized my name was not on any of the bank accounts Dave had opened during our marriage. And except when he shared information with me, I had no idea how our money was being spent. As I began asking questions about our finances, Dave became more and more defensive. He appeared to interpret my questioning and probing as a lack of trust in him. The more I insisted on disclosure, the angrier Dave became, and his way of dealing with these issues was to shut down and walk away without answering me. He was not accustomed to anyone questioning him. The more defensive Dave became, the more insecure I began to feel—especially since his name was on the deed of my house, which was my life's savings. Since we had never gotten around to the prenuptial I had wanted, my fears about the what-ifs and worst case began.

Blending our lives together in our fifties was so much harder than I ever imagined, especially because we jumped right in after only seven months! I was naïve to think because we shared so many of the same interests, our union would come naturally. Maybe our conflicts stemmed from being too much alike. Dave

LIFE IS A JOURNEY
AND IT IS LOVE
THAT MAKES
THAT JOURNEY
WORTHWHILE.

—UNKNOWN

and I were great together in so many ways, and I knew we loved one another; however, even too much of a good thing in a recipe will ruin it. We were many times too passionate, prideful, obsessive-compulsive, controlling, opinionated, and strong willed for our own good—type A, wanting to be right, and both as tenacious as our terriers.

There were two head chefs in our kitchen, in control and in charge, arguing over everything from how much money I spent to how to make the best homemade pizza! It sometimes seemed we were living in Hell's kitchen and not Hope Lane anymore. Everything was cooking on high and about to boil over.

Our recipe for love was turning into a recipe for disaster as I realized I had married a male Martha Stewart (Mark). And Lord knows there can only be one Martha! Our miscommunication and love-language differences created the fireworks that tested my faith, bringing me again to my knees in prayer. Our power struggles over finances were becoming more frequent and more volatile as I continued questioning Dave, now demanding to see all of our financial statements.

Why don't I have access to these accounts, and why isn't my name on these accounts? All of these important issues should have been dealt with way before marriage, absolutely before refinancing, and definitely before remodeling and combining all our savings.

"Should have, could have, would have . . ." I have a pantry full.

Dave's threats of leaving the marriage when I would demand answers or question our finances, telling me I was being "too controlling," caused my old insecurities and fears to surface once again. I needed to end my recurring fear of lack of finances, fear of failure, and deep-rooted insecurities once and for all. I was so tired of putting this baggage down at one terminal only to pick it up again at the next.

Knowledge became the power I needed with prayer as my power source.

I began by seeking legal counsel to learn about my rights within the community of our marriage. (After three marriages, you'd think I'd have it memorized by now!) But I loved being married, and I had never entered into marriage thinking of an exit plan. The legal rights I discovered I had gave me a glimmer of hope.

I polished up my résumé and found a wonderful full-time job opportunity if I wanted it, which would offer me both financial security and travel opportunities. I started to feel more confident about my future.

I was committed to my personal growth as well; I began rereading books from my counseling reconfirming what I already knew. Our marital disagreements and power struggles had nothing to do with money but everything to do with our common issues of trust, safety, and security. (Lord, I asked for my match, not my twin!)

On Valentine's weekend five years after our very first date, these common themes from our past came to a head. After another intense argument surrounding trust and finances, boundaries were crossed with threats of separation and even divorce. I left our house that evening feeling anxious as I drove to my sister's and ended up staying the night. Again, I surrendered everything to God: my fears of living life alone and my fears of making it financially, even letting go of my vision of hope (my house). I was determined to never again let my fears about finances influence me into making hasty decisions. I crawled into the guest bedroom exhausted and fell asleep as I meditated on God's faithfulness and how He had always provided for me.

As I headed home late that next morning, I was hoping to talk to Dave about starting counseling together so we could work things out, but when I walked through the door, my jaw dropped. I couldn't believe what I saw. Neatly stacked and marked boxes filled the living room, the dining room, Dave's office, and the garage.

Sixty-plus boxes were packed with everything from his tools to his mother's fine china and serving pieces. As I walked through our home, all I saw that remained was his closet of clothes, his large French armoire, buffet, and the antique bed we shared.

Dave looked exhausted as he walked over to me and told me he had been up all night packing. With tears in his eyes, he told me his movers were scheduled to arrive by noon. Quietly he said, "You can keep Harry and Sally with you."

I couldn't believe what I was hearing. It all felt surreal. I didn't want to fight anymore. I had surrendered my fears and was now ready to trust and accept whatever life would bring. I was ready to let Dave go if that's what he really wanted. *If Dave is this unhappy and doesn't love me or our life together enough to work on our marriage, than there is nothing more I can do. These problems we are facing are not insurmountable to me, but I guess they are to him.*

I went into my office and started crying and began praying. As crazy as everything was around me, I had a feeling of peace, even while hearing Dave's tape gun screeching over one box after the next.

I calmly called my sister. "Dave's moving out. Can you come over?"

She arrived just before the movers. As I opened the door to let her in, she put her arms around me and hugged me. "You're going to make it through this. You have so much to offer." I broke down. I was crying for the loss I was feeling, but I was no longer afraid. Debbie and I walked into my home office just as the movers arrived. We talked, prayed, laughed, and cried together as we watched Dave's boxes and my life with him disappear into the moving truck in front of our home.

When I went into my bedroom to get something, I found Dave crying. He stopped packing his clothes and came over to me, hugging me as if he never wanted to let go. As he held me, we both were sobbing.

Dave cried, "I don't want to do this. I don't want to leave you. I want my life with you."

I had never experienced these heartfelt feelings from Dave, much less heard him cry out tears from the deepest part of his soul. He was in so much pain.

"Why are you doing this, Dave?" I was bawling. "You don't have to choose fight or flight. We can work through this. Whatever you're running from will follow you where ever you go."

He just looked at me as he tried to compose himself. He began packing again. "I have to do this. I have no choice."

Wiping my tears, I walked out of our bedroom, passing the movers in the hall while they carried more of our life away.

I went back into my office and heard one of the movers yell, "Hey, Dave, we're ready for the big stuff now. Should we start movin' it on out? We need to start takin' apart them big pieces of yours." I overheard Dave tell them to take a cigarette break on the clock.

"No problem, man. It's your money, and you the boss," I heard one of the guys say.

Dave came into my office and asked me if we could talk. I agreed as he gently took my hand and walked me into our backyard that was filled with the many flowers and trees we had planted together and where we had shared so many fond memories with our family and friends. As we sat down together, Dave had tears in his eyes.

"What do you want me to do? I don't think you love me anymore. You always seem so mad at me. I can't do anything right any more."

By seeing Dave's vulnerability, I became vulnerable as well, and with tears in my eyes I responded to him. "I do love you, Dave. I love what a good provider you are and how hard you work and the way you take care of our home and can fix anything. I love how you help with the laundry, the cooking, and the grocery shopping and how you can turn a refrigerator of leftovers into a gourmet meal. I love that you like hanging out with our children and our families and that you send flowers to your mom on *your* birthday. I love how you talk to Harry and Sally when you brush them . . . and I especially love how safe and loved I feel when we cuddle together in bed while you whisper, 'this is the best part of my day.' And I love that you're not afraid or intimated by anything."

"Oh but I am," he interrupted. "I'm afraid of you at times and your need to control me. "

"Dave, I admit I have a hard time relinquishing control in many areas. I'm working on that. I've been in charge of raising two daughters and making it on my own in life for so long now, but believe me, I don't want to control you. I have a hard enough time controlling me. I've always been a strong-willed woman, and I spelled out everything I was looking for in my profile. You pursued me, remember? My profile said a one-hundred-one-hundred partnership and a mind, body, and soul connection. And that my man must be committed to personal and spiritual growth. Just going to church on Sunday is not spiritual growth. You do so many things right, Dave, but what we have together is not a true partnership or soul connection. The neck turns the head in most all great relationships, and you need to trust that I would never do anything to intentionally hurt you, because that would only hurt us." Dave wiped my tears with his handkerchief.

"We both have issues to deal with, and unless you are completely committed to counseling together, getting a postnuptial in place, and then sharing everything in our lives including your feelings and our finances, we don't have a chance of making it. Dave, I do believe God brought us together for a reason, and together with God's help we can work through our hurts to heal one another. There are books written about this, if you'll only take the time to read them. The choice is yours, Dave. I am not the one with the moving truck idling out front."

Dave just stared at me and listened without interrupting. For the longest time we just looked at each other saying nothing. After moments of silence, Dave said, "So you really want me to stay?"

"I do," I replied, "but only if you're committed to doing what-ever it takes."

He breathed a loud of sigh of relief, as if he had been holding his breath, then kissed me and took my hand as we walked out to the moving truck in front of our house. The movers were leaning up against the truck, smoking their cigarettes.

Dave said to them, "Well guys, I guess you'll need to bring all the boxes back into the house. We've decided to work things out."

Smiling from ear to ear, revealing the gaps between his cigarette-stained teeth, one of the movers exclaimed, "Hot damn, Leroy, I won the bet!" He continued, "I told my partner you two loved each other. You're not like the couple we just moved yesterday, with all their cussing and yelling and throwin' things. We was lucky to get out in one piece."

I laughed as we stood together at the back of their moving truck. Leroy leaned over and asked me, "Just how long you two been married?"

"We're going on our fifth year." I answered.

He laughed and said, "Why, you two are just figurin' things out. You need to give it some time 'cause you two are still in love. I can see it in your eyes."

My tears welled up as I looked over at Dave and saw tears in his eyes too.

He continued, saying, "Why me and my old lady have been together for twenty-some years now ,and let me tell you we do have us some fights but I never ever think of leaving her. I made a promise to her, and a real man don't ever back down on his promise."

I chuckled to myself as I stood there thinking of the irony of it all. Here Dave and I were finally getting couples counseling from complete strangers while standing in our front yard at the back of a moving truck. Maybe these movers weren't strangers at all, but angels in disguise. We'll never know.

On that tear-filled day, Dave and I made the decision to keep our marriage commitment, work on our relationship, and renew the love we knew we had for with each other. We needed a change of heart more than a change of address. And with God at the helm our relationship, we are rebuilding the foundation of our marriage and redefining our relationship.

Dave and I have begun counseling, and with legal help we are creating the nuptial agreement that we should have created before we married. Better late than never, as the saying goes. (Where did I hear that before?)

The conflict between us was the catalyst I needed to finally let go of my fears and to become more honest with myself, more honest with Dave, and closer to God. I now realize sometimes our trials are necessary to fulfill our calling, and it is the journey that makes us strong.

The silver lining and lesson is always there if you look for it.

God's never-failing love has been there for me throughout my entire life. His agape love is teaching me that the love and acceptance I have been searching for can never be found in another person but rather inside myself through His grace, His goodness, and His forgiveness. God is refining me into the woman of strength, courage, and grace He created me to be.

My partner cannot fill my voids or heal my hurts; only God's love can. Together God and I are filling the cracks and crevices of my heart with His healing balm of love.

By embracing His unconditional love, I finally know that I do not need a man in my life to complete or take care of me, no matter what the romance novels say. Instead, I choose to be with someone because I want to, not because I need to.

I have taken the rose-colored glasses off now. The fairytale ending doesn't exist, and the Cinderella story isn't real. But with total commitment, honesty, and work there can be a happily-ever-after.

Truth is liberating and brings the freedom for God to work all things together for good. God wants to surpass my dreams; I know that and believe that now.

At this time, Dave and I are committed to continue growing spiritually and emotionally—both together and individually. We are learning new love languages, new ways to love ourselves, and new ways to love one another.

My hope is that we will create a happily-ever-after ending "til death do us part" and a soul-satisfying recipe for a sweet and fulfilling life worth sharing with others.

Bentley—Our angel dog

Our Napa wedding

Third time's
a charm

LIFE INGREDIENT: LOVE
THIRD TIME'S A CHARM TRIPLE CHOCOLATE CHUNK BROWNIES

1 cup butter
1 cup granulated sugar
1 cup brown sugar
2 teaspoons vanilla
Small pinch of instant espresso coffee
4 large eggs, slightly beaten
1 cup all-purpose flour
¼ cup unsweetened cocoa powder
½ teaspoon salt
½ teaspoon baking powder
4 ounces semi-sweet chocolate chips or chunks
8 ounces bittersweet dark chocolate chopped coarsely
1 cup pecans or walnuts, chopped coarsely (optional)

➤ Preheat oven to 350 degrees.

➤ Grease a 13 x 9 inch pan and line with parchment paper.

➤ In medium bowl, mix all dry ingredients together. Reserve ¼ cup and toss semi-sweet chocolate chunks and nuts. Set aside.

➤ In medium saucepan over low heat, melt butter and bittersweet chocolate. Turn off heat, add sugar, vanilla, coffee and eggs; blend well. Stir in flour mixture and mix well.

➤ Add coated chocolate chunks with remaining flour mixture and nuts, stir to incorporate. Coating the chunks and chips keeps them from sinking to bottom of batter. Pour into prepared pan.

➤ Bake for 45-55 minutes or until set. Cool completely before cutting.

Makes 36 bars.

Enjoy!

LIFE INGREDIENT: LOVE
Doggie Cookies: BENTLEY BONES

2¼ cups whole wheat flour
¾ cup all-purpose flour
1 Tablespoon + ½ teaspoon
baking powder

1 teaspoon brown sugar
1¼ cup chunky peanut butter
1¼–1½ cups milk

➤ Preheat oven to 400 degrees.

➤ Line cookie sheet with parchment paper.

➤ Combine flours and baking powder in a large bowl, set aside.

➤ Combine peanut butter, sugar, and milk; beat until smooth.

➤ Gradually add flour mixture to wet ingredients until combined into a dough ball. If dough is crumbly, add more milk to combine.

➤ Turn dough onto a lightly floured surface and roll to about ¼ to ½ -inch thickness depending on desired thickness of cookie. Cut with bone shaped cookie cutter.

➤ Bake for 15-16 minutes, or until edges are lightly browned. (Cooking time will vary depending on thickness of cookie.)

➤ Cool before storing.

Your dog will love these almost as much as a tummy rub!

AFTERWORD

Courage, sacrifice, determination, commitment, toughness, heart, talent, guts. That's what little girls are made of; the heck with sugar and spice.

—Bethany Hamilton

As I look back over my life, I can see the loving hand of God gently guiding and encouraging me while honoring my passions, talents, and tenacity like a loving and supportive parent wanting so more for me for me than I could ever imagine. His ways are higher than ours and his timing is perfect.

For years, friends and family have asked me to create gourmet cookie dough that could be freshly baked, right in their own kitchen. I've dreamed of doing so since I opened my second Blue Chip store. But back then, the business experts told me there wasn't a demand for gourmet-quality refrigerated cookie dough. Well, twenty years later, I have once again decided that there will always be room for the best.

As my cookies were gobbled up by acquaintances at work and devoured by family and friends at gatherings, I was told regularly, "Lori, you should go back into the cookie business," and, "These are the best cookies I have ever tasted." Flattered, I just laughed.

While completing the dream of writing my book and telling my story, I've been creating recipes that were better than any I had ever devised. After months of experimenting, baking, and tasting hundreds of cookies, and gaining and losing the same six pounds, Lori's Legendary gourmet cookies and cookie dough will finally be available for you to enjoy at home.

Since 1983, my cookie creations have been copied by many companies, but never duplicated. Imitation is the best form of flattery, but imitation does not belong anywhere in my cookies. No nips, no tucks, no trans-fats. Nothing artificial, nothing imitation, just real, honest-to-goodness cookie dough created with a gourmet twist. And some varieties are gluten-free—only you'd never know it!

And my favorite part about Lori's Legendary is the privilege of giving back a portion of the sales to Hope Charities throughout the world.

My story and cookie passion has come full circle. My life is overflowing with an abundance of blessings as another dream comes true!

From my kitchen to your oven, The Cookie Queen is back with *Lori's Legendary Cookies!*

These are my best recipes ever! I hope you love them as much as I do!

With Blessings and Hope,

Lori Nader Gray

Visit my website at **www.Lorislegendary.com** to find out where you can purchase Lori's Legendary cookies and cookie dough and give back to Hope Charities.

ACKNOWLEDGEMENTS

There are so many people I want to thank for helping me complete my dream of writing my book. First of all, I would like to thank my parents, who have always believed in me and supported me, no matter how crazy or farfetched my ideas. Mom, without your love of baking and Dad, your insatiable sweet tooth, there may never have been Blue Chip Cookies. I love you both very much.

I also want to thank my sister and best friend, Debbie, who helped me with ideas and editing as we laughed, cried, and created cookies together as I obsessed over every detail. Sister, your love and friendship mean the world to me. And to my brother, Richard, whose gift of writing added tidbits of humor to my story. Your wit has always cracked me up. I laugh just thinking about our times together.

Thank you to Kim for helping me during the beginning drafts of my book. And Tom for your gift of graphic artistry, taking my vision for my Lori's Legendary logo and book cover and turning them into a beautiful reality. And Lori Hope, thank you for your tough editing and re-editing as I was writing my story, making me a better author in the process. Your belief in me and my message encouraged me to continue day after day.

And to Hal Donaldson for introducing me to the HigherLife Publishing Team: David Welday, Alice Bass, and Patti Reynolds. Thank you for your expertise, your encouragement, your prayers, and your honest feedback during the publishing process. And also to Ann Summer for doing such a wonderful job with the final editing of my story. You all feel like family now.

Thank you to all my girlfriends who have laughed and cried with me—with and without champagne. And special thanks to Rich McVey, my dear friend and talented photographer whose skill and expert eye for detail restored my photos and helped in creating the cover of my book.

And to Harry and Sally for keeping me company in my office at all hours of the day and night while writing my book.

Most importantly, thank you to my daughters, Adele and Lindsay, whose love and encouragement always inspired me to live with hope and pursue my dreams. I love you girls more than you will ever know. Never forget, "Dreams are illustrations from the book your soul is writing about you" (unknown author).

And of course, my husband, Dave, alias Mark Stewart, who supported and believed in me, knowing he could never stop this tenacious terrier, alias Cover Girl and Cookie Queen.

Thank you all for hearing my stories ad nauseam and taste-testing Lori's Legendary cookies, morning, noon, and night helping me to perfect my recipe.

You are all a blessing to me!

ENDNOTES

1. http://www.brainyquote.com/quotes/quotes/j/jimrohn109882. html (Accessed June 17, 2010)

2. http://www.brainyquote.com/quotes/quotes/t/theodorero125564. html (Accessed June 15, 2010)

3. http://www.goodreads.com/quotes/show/23014 (Accessed June 17, 2010)

4. http://www.motivational-and-famous-quotes.com/passion-quotes.html (Accessed June 17, 2010)

5. http://www.brainyquote.com/quotes/quotes/m/michelange108779.html (Accessed June 16, 2010)

6. http://www.inspirational-quotations.com/faith-quotes.html (Accessed June 16, 2010)

7. http://en.thinkexist.com/search/searchquotation.asp?search=Choose+a+job+you+love (Accessed June 16, 2010)

8. http://www.brainyquote.com/quotes/keywords/praying.html (Accessed June 16, 2010)

9. http://www.brainyquote.com/quotes/quotes/m/martinluth103425.html (Accessed June 17, 2010)

10. http://www.biblegateway.com/quicksearch/?quicksearch=Now+faith ı is ı bcing+surc&qs_version=NIV (Accessed June 17, 2010)

11. http://www.quotationspage.com/quote/25845.html (Accessed June 14, 2010)

12. http://en.thinkexist.com/search/searchquotation.asp?search=To+forgive+is+the+highest,+most+beautiful+form+of+love (Accessed June 16, 2010)

13. http://www.quotationspage.com/quote/258.html (Accessed June 16, 2010)

14. http://www.brainyquote.com/quotes/authors/s/saint_thomas_aquinas_3.html (Accessed June 16, 2010)

15. http://www.brainyquote.com/quotes/quotes/e/eleanorroo141470.html (Accessed June 17, 2010)

16. http://www.brainyquote.com/quotes/quotes/w/waltdisney163027.html (Accessed June 17, 2010)

17. http://www.brainyquote.com/quotes/quotes/h/helenkelle164579.html (Accessed June 17, 2010)

18. http://www.inspirational-quotations.com/faith-quotes.html (Accessed June 17, 2010)

19. http://www.brainyquote.com/quotes/quotes/o/orisonswet157900.html (Accessed June 17, 2010)

20. http://www.brainyquote.com/quotes/quotes/f/frankhowar105963.html (Accessed June 17, 2010)

21. http://www.brainyquote.com/quotes/quotes/e/eecummin161271.html (Accessed June 17, 2010)

22. http://www.favoritequotes.org/humor-quotes/347/ (Accessed June 17, 2010)

23. http://thinkexist.com/quotation/life_is_like_riding_a_bicycle-to_keep_your/327432.html (Accessed June 18, 2010)

24. http://drphil.com/articles/article/230 (Accessed June 18, 2010)

25. http://www.brainyquote.com/quotes/quotes/m/marcustull122152.html (Accessed June 18, 2010)

26. http://www.quotegarden.com/gratitude.html (Accessed June 18, 2010)

27. http://en.thinkexist.com/quotation/we_come_to_love_not_by_finding_a_perfect_person/198409.html (Accessed June 19, 2010)

28. http://en.thinkexist.com/quotation/where_there_is_great_love-there_are_always/149993.html (Accessed June 19, 2010)

DON'T KEEP MY BOOK A SECRET!

- **Become My Friend, Follower, & Fan**: Keep up with the latest "Lori Story" by becoming my Facebook Friend or Fan and Twitter Follower. I'll send you regular updates on my speaking events, book discounts, as well as my business buzz.

- **Share With Your Friends**: Tell your friends what you liked about *From Cover Girl to Cookie Queen* on your blog, Twitter, Facebook, or any other social network account.

- **The Perfect Gift**: *From Cover Girl to Cookie Queen* makes a perfect gift, especially for bridal showers, birthdays, or Mother's Day.

- **Help Me Get My Book in the Bookstores**: Because *From Cover Girl to Cookie Queen* is available through all of the major distributors, bookstores can order it conveniently. So if you don't see my book on the shelf, be sure to order it. The greater the demand, the higher the chances *From Cover Girl to Cookie Queen* will make some bookstore shelf space.

- **Give Me a Raving Review**: If you purchased *From Cover Girl to Cookie Queen* through Amazon.com (or even if you didn't), you can write a raving review for my book! This provides fantastic publicity!

- **Key Connections**: If you know of an organization, business, school, or association, that would be interested in using *From Cover Girl to Cookie Queen* as a resource, contact my publisher immediately!

HigherLife Publishing: media@ahigherlife.com

CONNECT WITH ME...

- **Radio, Television, & Newspaper**: If you work in radio, television or newspaper, invite me for an interview! You'll find me to be a delightful, entertaining guest!

- **Public Speaking**: I always make special time for special invitations, so if you'd like for me to come and share my story at your work or church or for your special organization, please contact me!

To learn more about *From Cover Girl to Cookie Queen* please contact me at: **lori@lorislegendary.com**.

You may also contact my publisher directly:

HigherLife Publishing
400 Fontana Circle
Building 1 – Suite 105
Oviedo, Florida 32765
Phone: (407) 563-4806
Email: media@ahigherlife.com

THE COOKIE QUEEN IS BACK!
With cookies to satisfy your sweet tooth and your soul...

When Lori went from a hope filled Cover Girl to Cookie Queen she make cookie history in 1983 by creating the first White Chocolate Macadamia Nut Cookie. It was love at first bite. Now she's back and giving back with Lori's Legendary Cookies!

WHEN YOU ORDER FROM LORI'S LEGENDARY YOU WILL SATISFY YOUR SWEET TOOTH.....

> With every incredible bite you will savor the taste of creamy butter, Madagascar bourbon vanilla, melt in your mouth Guittard chocolate and delicious nuts and fruits.

> We bake with the finest locally sourced ingredients and each of Lori's Legendary cookies is made from scratch in small batches by hand to guarantee freshness.

AND YOU WILL SATISFY YOUR SOUL....

Each order of cookies comes with an inspirational quote card from one of Lori's 10 Life ingredients, and all our packaging is 100% recyclable.

But the most satisfying part is knowing that your order of Lori's Legendary Cookies will be helping Hope Charities throughout the world.

Go to **www.LorisLegendary.com** to order the Incredibly Indulgent:

- White Wripple Chunk
- Toffee Chip Royale
- White Lemon Dreams
- Outrageous Oatmeal Raisin
- And more....